D0843966

THE INTENTIONAL LIFE

THE INTENTIONAL LIFE

REFLECTIONS FROM CONSCIOUS LIVING

MEREDITH WHIPPLE CALLAHAN

POTRERO PRESS

For my wife, Liz, and my friend, Mike,
who read every word along the way

Published by Potrero Press, Norwalk, Connecticut
www.potreropress.com

Cover design by Noel Lee
Interior design by Sarah Beaudin
ISBN: 9781733693608
e-ISBN: 9781733693615

First edition

CONTENTS

PREFACE

My blog, *The Intentional*, launched in May 2014 while I was visiting the Kloster Arenberg, a convent outside of Frankfurt, Germany. I was then—and continue to be—a junkie for solitary, spiritual retreats. At the time, nothing sounded better than a quiet weekend amongst nuns. Between walks in the woods, visits to the stations of the cross, and trips to the sauna, I managed to write my first post—all 518 words of it.

In that first entry, "The Courage to Begin," I expressed anxiety that my writing would not be good enough, and that posts shared on the web would be hauntingly permanent. But more than either of those fears, I feared the judgment of others. I wrote, "There's vulnerability in expressing myself authentically... What if you think I'm silly, stupid, or too much of a hippie? What if you think I'm too pragmatic, too intellectual, or not intuitive enough?" While I was theoretically bought in on authenticity, I dreaded its ramifications both online and in real life.

Yet, over the last five years and seventy-five posts, I continued to put myself out there. With each post, I learned more about myself. With each post, I came to care less about the opinions of others. Just as important, with each post, I came to understand more about what mattered to me. As I moved away from worrying about approval, I focused more and more on my mission: to give a clearer view to life and how to live it meaningfully. Now, I have the courage not only to publish my work online, but also to share the collective wisdom of *The Intentional* in this book.

Which brings us to *The Intentional Life*. As I worked through this manuscript, I realized how very personal this book is. With the exception of the chapter introductions (which reflect my thinking), the bulk of the book reflects my living. So, before you start reading, I think it only fitting that you get to meet me.

THE AUTHOR

I'm Meredith. I grew up in Port Huron, Michigan, a small town in the shadow of the auto industry to the South and Canada to the East. I benefited from a cozy community in which both parents, my brother, and all four grandparents could attend my enthusiastic but non-competitive figure skating performances. When I was admitted to Yale, I felt like I had won the lottery; in many ways, that was true. Since school, my career has been in the business world, initially as a strategy consultant doing whatever offered the steepest learning curve, but increasingly in the leadership development space where my heart remains today. I believe leadership is just the word that businesses use to get comfortable with all the important stuff that happens within and between people.

Though my career has been spent in business, I've always had a spiritual underbelly. I was most excited to get a car at sixteen so I could drive myself to church. In another life, I would have been a minister. I have variously been a Bible-reading Episcopal, a would-be Jew jealous of every gorgeous ritual, a justice-seeking Unitarian Universalist, and a guru-following yogi. Regardless, I am someone who seeks truth, light, and love in whatever form. My superpower in this life is loving people unconditionally.

Integrating both these dimensions of myself is one of my biggest personal struggles. How do the parts of myself that yearn to be respected as smart, logical, and traditionally accomplished coexist with the parts of myself that are more authentic, intuitive, and spiritual? I am most afraid that I am too hippie for the businesspeople and too business for the hippies. And yes, I do eat a lot of kale.

I have mostly dated men and am married to the most remarkable woman, Liz. She is a Black Hawk MEDEVAC pilot turned healthcare professional who is braver, more loyal, more observant, more dedicated, more playful, and more romantic than anyone I have ever met. She's an incredible parent. When I am stuck in a tough Mommy moment, I always ask myself, *WWLD? What would Liz do?* Together, we have two children, Elliott Claire (a lady-toddler with wild hair, a big imagination, and a ridiculous vocabulary) and Hawk (a chubby and chill gentleman-newborn and a bundle of love).

I struggle with tendencies towards perfectionism, competitiveness, and control. I can be paralyzed by my desire for approval, my need for inclusion, and my awkwardness around authority. As my wife will affirm, I am a mediocre driver with a terrible sense of direction and inferior taste in music, the combination of which makes me useless on a road trip. I have the memory of a goldfish.

That said, I am reflective by nature, to which my boxes upon boxes of journals will testify. I dictated my earliest journal entries to my mother, who transcribed the events of kindergarten in her flawless handwriting. Over time, my journals became the territory of penning terrible teenage poetry, processing new college experiences, and stepping into adult decision-making. Today, journaling has become my constant companion for self-reflection and personal evolution. These reflective tendencies are manifest on every page of *The Intentional Life*.

My purpose in life is to bring clarity. With clarity comes choice. And, when I'm living up to my ambitions, with choice comes intentionality. I write books about these topics because it's the best way for me to come to clarity for myself and to be of service to others.

This is me—or at least what I know of me so far.

This introduction aside, ultimately this book is not so much about me. Yes, it is a series of personal essays that you can now contextualize in my broader life. But even as I share myself, I know that I am not the focus. This book is actually about our common life—and the opportunity to live that life intentionally. It is simply seen and articulated through my lens.

GOALS OF THE BOOK

I have two goals for this book. My first goal is that you have a rich, personal encounter with intentional living, one that changes not only the way you look at life, but also the way you live it. My second goal is that this book provides the foundation to enter, together, into a deeper collective discussion of the topic. So, if you find the book meaningful, please share it with a friend or three. And if you are not yet a subscriber to *The Intentional*, you can sign up on the website (www.theintentional.net) to receive new essays in your inbox.

As always, I am delighted to hear from you and look forward to being in rich dialogue about many of these ideas. You can always reach me via my website: www.meredithwhipplecallahan.com.

I wish you a deep reflective experience of this book, and, more importantly, an intentional life.

With love and gratitude,
Meredith Whipple Callahan
Norwalk, Connecticut
May 2019

INTRODUCTION

From time to time, I find myself winding my way through life incidentally. I am surprised to find that I just spent the last two hours of my life on Facebook. I realize that I just ate a whole pint of ice cream without tasting it. Or even worse, entire weeks go by during which I make major life decisions—about work, about home, about relationships—without much reflection.

When I started my blog, *The Intentional*, this was my paranoia: that I would live life incidentally instead of intentionally. Further, I was afraid that, over time, those incidental actions would accumulate, so much so that they would create my values, form my beliefs, and, ultimately, shape my identity.

This is not a crazy or unfounded fear. It's not uncommon that we do any number of things in our lives—from small, daily actions to big, sweeping decisions—with less thought than would be ideal. As recent science shows, this lack of consideration comes, in part, from the overwhelming cognitive burden we bear. Given the amount of information we're assaulted by, we cannot hyper-analyze each of our actions and still make it through the day. Yet, I have to believe that I—and that we—can do better than letting ourselves operate so automatically.

To some extent, this thoughtlessness exists because the collective "we" have yet to name it as a problem. We have not pointed our finger at thoughtlessness and found it guilty. We have not looked around for its alternative. Furthermore, we have not identified the alternative and given it a name.

I have. I call it intentionality.

WHAT IS INTENTIONALITY?

Colloquially when we say, "That was intentional," we mean that we did something on purpose. We mean that we did it consciously. We mean that we hoped for the intended effect. We take responsibility for the action and all its consequences.

The formal concept of intentionality is simply an expansion of this everyday idea. Intentionality is consciously aligning *what you do* with *what you want*. Let me say that again because it bears repeating. Intentionality is consciously aligning *what you do* with *what you want*. As such, living intentionally revolves around asking two deceptively simple questions: *What do you want?* and *What are you doing?*

On one hand, you need to think through *What do I want?* There are all sorts of variations upon this theme. What do you want to achieve? What kind of a person do you want to be? What impact do you want to have on others and on the world? In sum, what kind of a life do you want to lead? This is the realm of core values, life purpose, and big goals. Reflecting upon these questions prompts you to articulate a conscious vision of what you want to create in yourself and beyond yourself.

At the same time, you need to grapple with *What am I doing?* This is the realm of the mundane and the everyday. Consider: What would someone see if they videotaped your life and played it back on mute? How would they see you spending your time? Who would they see you associating with? Without more information, who would they deduce you are? And, most important, would what they see align with what you said you wanted?

Ultimately, the questions of *What do I want?* and *What am I doing?* converge in the question of *What am I becoming?* To quote a line often attributed to Aristotle, "We are what we repeatedly do." You are the collection of your actions in the world. Every day, by acting in certain ways and not in others, you create certain habits, cultivate certain skills, develop certain personality traits, and engrain certain beliefs. This is true not only in major matters such as how you spend your time, how you treat others, and what you contribute to the world, but equally in seemingly more mundane matters such as what you eat, what you buy, and what you wear. Your entire identity is nothing more than the sum of your choices in each moment. Each action, whether intentional or not, forms you.

Stepping back, I find it crazy that we, myself included, are the accidental byproducts of our experiences. By letting ourselves be incidentally formed, we cede our decision-making power to a combination of the least evolved parts of our brains and the outside influences that would take advantage of them. The earliest part of our brain to evolve, known as the reptilian brain, causes us to act automatically and without thinking, often driven by a combination of emotion, instinct, and pattern-recognition. When operating unconsciously, we also allow the habits established by our previous choices to run automatically and determine the course of our lives. In this mode, our choices are heavily subject the world around us, taking cues from advertising and fake news, from peer pressure and societal norms. Ultimately, all this leaves little room for the higher-level cognition that characterizes intentionality.

This continues to be true until you awaken to living consciously. You see the inner drivers—the mindsets, emotions, and norms—that influence not only your choices but also your very perception. You differentiate between your ambitions for yourself and the outside influences that might sway you. You see how your everyday actions create your identity. Over time, you start to consciously choose the actions that align with your ambitions. You determine what you become. And, if you do it well, you are able to act as the author of your own life.

WHAT WILL I GET OUT OF *THE INTENTIONAL LIFE*?

It is one thing to define intentionality and another to put it into practice. I do not have all the answers on how to live perfectly with full intention. I can, however, provide you a clear definition of intentionality and a series of vivid examples showing its application in my own life.

I hope that, after reading *The Intentional Life*, you will see more clearly. You will know what intentionality is and be able to identify it in the world. You will see how your actions do (or don't) align with what you want. And, you will learn more about yourself. If this book has done its job, by the time you put it down, you will be awakened, called, and inspired to live your life more consciously—and to encourage others to do the same.

To be clear, when you close this book, the work will not be done. On the contrary, it will be just beginning. Intentionality is a value, and, like other values, it takes effort, active effort, to honor it in our lives. But this is essential work to do. We need to move more intentionally—individually and collectively—if we are to both create the lives we want and to work together to re-form humanity toward a new vision. This book marks the beginning of that journey.

HOW IS THE BOOK ORGANIZED?

The Intentional Life is a collection of personal essays originally published on my blog, *The Intentional.* I selected these thirty-four essays to give you a robust experience of living intentionally on a day-to-day basis. Each essay offers a window into a specific moment within the last five years of my life. I begin that period as a thirty-three-year-old San Franciscan, traveling the world for work and dating Liz, the woman I would soon marry. I end that period living in commuter-ville Connecticut with my wife, toddler daughter, and newborn son, trying to navigate the waters of early parenthood. In each situation, I try to become more aware, to reflect more deeply, to align my actions and my ambitions, and to surrender to the process. Living intentionally is hard, and I do not have it right. I struggle and fail and try again. I want you to see those aspects of my struggle with full vulnerability so that you may not only live more consciously, but also be gentle with yourself when you fail to do so.

These essays are not ordered chronologically but are instead organized into four sections, each one reflecting an emergent theme of intentional living. Chapter One, *Awareness,* focuses on the initial spark of new consciousness that allows you to see previously unseen forces in yourself and the world. Chapter Two,

Reflection, shows how reflection is an invaluable tool to dig into your lived experiences and to clarify what you want. Chapter Three, *Alignment,* investigates the core, constant challenge of living intentionally—the act of aligning what you do with what you want. And, perhaps paradoxically, Chapter Four, *Surrender,* presents an essential counterbalance to the controlling tendencies that are both encouraged by—and get in the way of—intentionality. I do not mean to present these dimensions as a linear, four-step plan. Instead, take these four chapters as persistent themes worthy of consideration. Use them to understand intentionality more deeply. Then, craft your own tailored approach to living intentionally, one that focuses on the aspects of intentionality that are most in need of attention in your life.

HOW SHOULD I APPROACH THIS BOOK?

There is no right way to read this book. While my editors and I put great effort into curating the collection and crafting a compelling trajectory, feel free to navigate yourself through the book. Read the book from front to back, or skip to the topics that compel you and the chapters that call to you. These essays were all originally published as standalone pieces, so it is easy to read them independently. Make the experience yours.

Inasmuch as this book is intended to prompt insight and change, I also invite you to pause and reflect. To facilitate this, I have added reflection questions at the end of each essay for you to engage more deeply. It's not important that my reflections feel true to you. You need not agree with them. Instead, I hope that by reading my reflections and then engaging in the questions, you see yourself more clearly.

To support reflection, you may also find it useful to read this book with a journal nearby and a pen in hand. In my experience, externalizing your reflection via writing, instead of simply thinking to yourself, yields better insights. Instead of a journal and pen, you can equally use a laptop, phone, or whatever format you find effective. I prefer writing by hand because it invites me to slow down and creates a space for self-reflection that is hard to access with other technologies.

In addition to going inside yourself to reflect, I also encourage you to go beyond yourself and discuss. Do not stop after reading these ideas. Talk about them as well. Bringing greater intentionality to life is easier when done with others.

WHAT ELSE?

Embedded in the very concept of intentionality is an understanding that you are the co-creator of your existence. The choices that you make on a day-to-day basis matter immensely. You are more powerful than you know, and you have more control over your life than you exercise. You set your vision and ambitions. You choose the values you honor. And, most important, you choose your actions. Start today by stepping back, choosing what to do next, and beginning to create your own intentional life.

CHAPTER ONE
AWARENESS

Without awareness, we all live in a reactive state. Actions in the world elicit reactions within us. We act without seeing the invisible forces that direct us away from one action and toward another. We act without consideration of what we want and without realizing the consequences of what we are becoming. As a result, we lose our identity in the context of what surrounds us.

Awakening to conscious living rarely happens all at once. Instead, if you endeavor to see things differently, your awareness slowly grows over time. You gain consciousness of the previously unseen forces driving your behavior. This includes everything from your emotions to your mindsets, from your biases to your fears. Beyond this, you also become aware of an increasing sense of choice in how you act. Awareness opens up the possibility of not automatically reacting, but consciously responding to situations. The automatic drivers of your behavior are short-circuited. Instead, you are able to create a pause in which you see things more clearly, navigate through the influences within you, and choose your actions.

Each of the essays included in this chapter tackles one of those inner drivers—mindsets, emotions, norms, and the like—and examines how that dimension is brought to awareness in everyday life.

AWARENESS OF EMOTIONS

This essay introduces the idea of responding to our circumstances instead of reacting to them. When we start to awaken to our lives, we begin to see choices where none existed before.

AUGUST 7, 2014
SAN FRANCISCO, CALIFORNIA

Every time I take Reese, our pup, to the dog park, he's terribly excited. There are dogs and people and more dogs and more people, and they all smell so interesting and different. Forget playing fetch or running around. Smelling is hands-down his favorite activity. Sometimes, he even smells so hard that he forgets to breathe and, as a result, starts to drool. Unfortunately, this little drool-faced pup reminds other owners of a rabid, frothing-at-the-mouth dog. So, in short, Reese loves to smell so much that other dogs and people think he's completely crazy. I say with pride: That's our dog.

I have learned to expect this reaction when I take him out. So, when we arrive at the park, I do the same thing every time. I tell him "sit" and "stay." Then I take off his leash and walk a step away. I remind him once more to "stay," at which point, he looks at me with a face full of agony and restraint. Finally I tell him, "Okay, go!" which means he can run around, diving into the smorgasbord of smells.

Lately, Reese has not been waiting that patient, disciplined second before I tell him to go. I remove the leash, and he's headed straight for the nearest dog's rear.

While frustrating, this morning's sprint for the smells prompted not only the appropriate discipline, but also a moment of self-reflection. Whether you're a dog like Reese or a human like me:

Emotions don't equal actions.

Being mad doesn't mean you yell.

Being sad doesn't mean you cry.

And being overcome by smells doesn't mean you run off.

Like Reese, I find myself using emotions as an excuse for my automatic behaviors. For example, while waiting in line at the Indian consulate recently, I told myself it made sense that I was annoyed because their process was inefficient. Before I knew it, I was speaking in an overly sharp tone and with an annoyed attitude to the woman behind the counter. But with good reason, right? We have a whole host of these actions that are collectively accepted in our culture as normal behavior:

- "I'm annoyed by your inefficient process…" (and therefore I'm allowed to be demanding and impatient)
- "I'm busy with more important things…" (and therefore I'm allowed to be less present and distracted around you)
- "I'm tired…" (and therefore I'm allowed to be crabby)

These are just excuses for our thoughtless behavior. We often act as if an external situation creates an internal state that dictates our actions—and that all of that is completely understandable, fair, and outside our control.

However reasonable my emotions and actions seem to be in a situation, I always have choice in the emotion I show and in the actions I choose. Especially when I have seemingly fantastic rationale of why I can justifiably be terrible to others, it's even more important to remember that little moment of choice.

I'm reminded of one my roommates in business school. After a strong night out, most of us would show up to class looking like hell and not very pleasant to be around. He, on the other hand, would look interview-ready in business formal. For most of us, there was an obvious, necessary causal relationship between our hangover and our haggard appearance. But he would get up, give himself a close shave, and dress in a proper suit. We all may have felt equally terrible those mornings, but he chose to do something completely different with the same feeling. He didn't buy into the easy, collective belief that a hangover gives you an excuse.

Emotions don't equal actions.

This realization isn't new. I've practiced non-reactivity in meditation classes. I've read countless books on mindfulness. I even train on the concept of presence in my day job. For every hackneyed insight and inspirational quote I spend a minute reading, there is a multi-month, multi-year, probably life-long process of internalizing, personalizing, and embodying that realization. The process is neither linear nor unidirectional. I try and try again, I fail and fail again, I realize and realize again. My challenge isn't understanding it intellectually. My challenge is living it.

This morning's walk in the dog park brought me a bit closer to remembering that my emotions don't control me. Both Reese and I can choose how we act, even when there's a really good rationale for acting in a certain way (just look at all those dogs!). I'm sure we'll both forget that—and have to learn it all over again—before the next time we return to the dog park.

Do you feel subject to your emotions or in control of them?

What situations or triggers lead you to have a more automatic, emotional reaction?

How can you remind yourself to take some space before responding?

AWARENESS OF HABITS

Over the course of your life, you create habits—habits of action, but also habits of thought—that come to form you. One of the major patterns that has driven me over the course of my life is a striving for comparative success, excellence, and perfection. Uncovering and understanding your patterned ways of thinking is the initial awareness that allows you to start to act differently.

FEBRUARY 5, 2015
SAN DIEGO, CALIFORNIA

It was only an off-handed comment, but I remember it clearly.

It was around 1997, and I was in high school. Specifically, I was hosting a dinner party at my parents' house (I was an interesting kid; who does that sixteen?). I set the table, carefully arranged the linens according to my recent studies of napkin-folding, and cooked up three different pasta dishes as a sort of pasta bar. I was chatting with one of my guests when she turned to me and delivered bluntly, "You know, Meredith, if not for one thing, I would want your life."

I felt wonderfully validated by the compliment. *You want my life?* I thought. *Well, then I must be doing something right!* My ego was satisfied. But, beyond that, I became immediately fixated on this one exception. *Wait! What part of my life could she judge and find wanting? I should definitely fix that right away.*

Much of my early years were spent striving to perfect myself. I worked hard in school for academic achievement, certainly studying more than necessary to get along. I poured myself into an appropriately diverse and engaging set of extracurriculars. Yet, my definition of achievement wasn't focused on resume-building alone. In addition to being the smartest and most accomplished, I wanted to be the most well-rounded too. I journaled about my experiences and cultivated my capacity for self-reflection. I built emotional intelligence skills around listening and connecting. I committed to reading the Bible every morning and night as I plumbed for spiritual depth.

Although I had a broad view of life, I had only one metric to measure every dimension against: excellence. Was I getting A's on tests, devotedly going to the gym, cultivating both breadth and depth in my relationships, calling my parents, and taking on leadership roles? Was I being the best? My goal was to do everything required to become a so-called complete human being and to do it all well. I would know I was on track if people looked at my life and, like my friend, said, "Gosh, I want what she has."

This worldview comes with plenty of issues. To begin, this perspective set me on an endless quest with predictably unsatisfying results. I learned that there will always be someone who is smarter, funnier, more empathetic, better-read, or more well-rounded. It's tough to be good at *one* thing, and it's much tougher to be the best at *all* things. Given that I didn't always find myself at the top of the heap, I also had to become an agile mental gymnast to preserve my sense of self-worth. I looked for ways to reestablish my identity when I lacked hard proof of relative superiority (like test grades). One trick was to subtly reframe and recontextualize what types of excellence really mattered. "Yes, it's important to be smart and emotionally intelligent like me," I would tell myself, "but it's not that important to have a great fashion sense or win at chess. So, in a way, I'm still the best." I picked the constellation of things that I would judge on, which meant that I could still define myself as comparatively better in any range of situations.

Although this worldview drove my achievements and gave me worth, I soon realized these subconscious patterns didn't help me connect with others. It's no fun to sit in a room silently cataloguing the reasons why I'm smarter than this person, more engaged than that person, or more emotionally aware than the other person. I didn't want to be constantly striving for more or perpetually reframing why my slate of achievements was better than the next person's.

So, I'm working on giving up those old habit patterns. I'm redefining success away from "excellence, comparative superiority, and desirability" to simply "authenticity." I used to make authenticity a sub-goal of my overarching quest to be the best (i.e., "Goal 915: Be the most authentic person around"). But I know it's far more powerful when authenticity becomes the dominant lens. Who am I? What is innately valuable about me? And how do I sit with all the parts of me instead of trying to perfect them? Frankly, I don't want you to covet my life. Instead, I want you to live *your* life more fully, just as I want to live *my life* fully. With all its real messiness and imperfection.

This focus on authenticity starts to neuter my reliance on external validation. I began my journey with a sense that if I made myself good enough, then others would want my life; they would like me, and I would have done well. But do you remember my friend from high school and her one reservation about wanting my life? She said she would love to be me except… "you worry too much." And so, as I throw out the idea of perfecting my life, I'll also throw out my biggest worry about doing so: the fear that unless I make myself better and better, then I might not be worthy of your love and approval. Hopefully, striving for authenticity means that love and approval don't need to come from you anymore. I should be able to find them in myself.

It's so easy for me, for any of us, to present only the Facebook veneer of a sublimated life: the travels, the engagements, the meals, the beach days with impossibly beautiful California weather. But regardless of what you see on your smartphone, here is the truth. I am not perfect. There is messiness and brokenness and not-all-put-together-ness in me. Far from being something I need to polish and perfect, I am more and more embracing the imperfect parts and loving myself through it all. It has taken me until my early thirties, but I have learned that I don't so much want to excel at life. I just want to live it.

What do you strive for (consciously or unconsciously)? Do you strive to be perfect? Well-liked? Smart? Right? Well-rounded? Relatable? Something else?

How does that striving benefit you?
How does that striving hold you back?

What does it look like for you
to live more authentically?

AWARENESS OF MINDSETS

Although this essay is more conceptual than personal, it introduces an essential topic: mindsets. Mindsets are the hidden operators that invisibly determine what's possible and impossible, what's good and bad, what's admirable and shameful in your world. The first step toward shifting your mindsets to be in your service is simply seeing them clearly. The following essay presents a useful framework for exposing your fundamental mindsets.

MARCH 29, 2016
SAN FRANCISCO, CALIFORNIA

I recently re-read Carol Dweck's book, *Mindset*. She argues that one orientation—an individual's relationship to growth—underlies nearly all aspects of life. If someone adopts a *growth mindset*, he believes his abilities (and those of others) can develop through dedication and hard work. If someone adopts a *fixed mindset*, he believes his abilities are unchangeable; one is born with abilities, and those determine his success. Dweck's argument states that nearly all metrics for success—everything from productivity to quality of relationships—are positively correlated with a growth mindset.

Happily, this work brought mindsets into the public consciousness in a bigger way. However, Dweck's focus on the growth/fixed mindset alone limits what mindsets can help us see. Ultimately, only a handful of foundational mindsets drive our orientation to the world. Surprising as this may seem, all our many differences are built upon only a handful of foundational beliefs.

WHAT ARE MINDSETS?

You can think of mindsets as the mega-beliefs underlying human existence. People have many small beliefs like "Putting the forks handle-side-down in the dishwasher is an unforgiveable sin" or "Boy Scouts have a strong moral compass." But the mindsets I'm talking about are bigger than those. They are fundamental orientations to the world upon which many of our functional, everyday beliefs are built. These mindsets are the topics of heated philosophical debates, the common understandings of political parties, and the cornerstones of many of the world's religions.

WHAT ARE THE FOUNDATIONAL MINDSETS?

I see thirteen foundational mindsets, split into two categories: mindsets about how the world works and mindsets about how you engage with that world. This list is not exhaustive, but it includes the most salient mindsets in my experience. For each of the thirteen dimensions there are two opposing beliefs that sit on either end of a spectrum. This depiction is artificially polarizing, however; anyone may hold one mindset, the opposite mindset, or paradoxically both at the same time.

MINDSETS ABOUT HOW THE WORLD WORKS

TRUTH	ABSOLUTE *"Truth is universal"*	←——————→	RELATIVE *"It depends"*
HUMAN NATURE	EVIL *"People are bad"*	←——————→	GOOD *"People are good"*
STRUCTURE	LOGICAL *"Everything is explainable"*	←——————→	MAGICAL *"The world is full of mystery"*
MEANING	RANDOM *"The world is driven by chance"*	←——————→	PURPOSEFUL *"Everything happens for a reason"*
POSSIBILITY	PESSIMISTIC *"Things generally don't work out"*	←——————→	OPTIMISTIC *"Things generally work out"*
EQUALITY	DIFFERENTIATED *"Some of us are better than others"*	←——————→	DISTINCT *"We all have unique talents"*
AVAILABILITY	LACKING *"There is not enough"*	←——————→	ABUNDANT *"There is plenty"*

MINDSETS ABOUT HOW I ENGAGE IN THE WORLD

CHANGE	FIXED *"I am who I am"*	←——————→	FLEXIBLE *"I can change over time"*
DESTINY	PRE-DETERMINED *"My path is chosen for me"*	←——————→	CHOICEFUL *"I choose my way"*
CONTROL	EXTERNAL *"I am not in charge"*	←——————→	INTERNAL *"I am in charge"*
FORCE	EFFORTFUL *"I need to work hard to succeed"*	←——————→	EFFORTLESS *"Things come easily"*
SUFFICIENCY	MAXIMIZING *"I seek the best"*	←——————→	SATISFYING *"I seek something good enough"*
OPPORTUNITY	LIMITED *"That won't work"*	←——————→	POSSIBLE *"I am open to trying"*

Foundational Mindsets

Because these dimensions are fundamental, all sorts of beliefs are built off them. For example, your mindset around availability (i.e., your sense of whether the world is fundamentally abundant or lacking) can inform your sense of self-worth (e.g., feeling like you are enough or not enough), your financial decisions (e.g., saving more or spending more), and your opinions on tax policy (e.g., redistributing income versus not). Each mindset impacts your relationship with self, your relationship with others, and your relationship with the world.

HOW DO I UNDERSTAND (AND MAYBE EVEN SHIFT) MY OWN MINDSETS?

Read through the foundational mindsets above a second time and assess yourself. Ask yourself the following:

- For each pair, under which mindset do I most commonly operate?
- Was this a conscious choice, or did I adopt it without consideration?
- Where did this mindset come from? Are there patterns of mindsets that come from my family, my religion, my culture, or my country? What, in my experience, leads me to operate under this mindset?

- When I hold this mindset, how do I act?

[Note: Our mindsets are often so ingrained that we see them as universals. For the purposes of this exercise, you might find it useful to adopt a *relative* orientation around the dimensions, allowing yourself to at least consider the possibility of the opposite mindset.]

After assessing the way that foundational beliefs show up in your life, ask the question, *What is the most productive mindset for me to hold?* Dweck argues throughout her book that we can choose our mindset, suggesting that people can develop the capacity to choose a growth mindset, even if their habits and conditioning incline them to hear the "fixed mindset voice" in their heads. You are similarly able to choose your mindset along any of these dimensions. Essentially, you can intentionally build the set of foundational mindsets that best enable you to get what you want.

What are my mindsets?

To what extent are these mindsets true?
To what extent are these mindsets useful to me?

What mindsets do I want to hold?

AWARENESS OF BIASES

Of all the drivers seen through increased awareness, biases are perhaps the most pernicious. Biases shift the way we perceive the world around us. Without our knowing it, they screw with our very cognition, bending our perception of reality through their lens. Greater awareness helps us to see how they operate within us even if we are not always able to avoid them.

NOVEMBER 1, 2015

SAN FRANCISCO, CALIFORNIA

Living in San Francisco, it's not uncommon that I hitch an Uber when I need to get around the city.

Debates on Uber continue to make headlines. How should we regulate ride-sharing? Is riding with a stranger safe? Is Uber's surge pricing just? How does ride-sharing impact congestion? Is the company's culture so problematic that we should boycott the service?

While these controversies swirl in my head, I know one thing to be true. Intended or not, Uber is healing the world, one ride at a time.

It sounds crazy, but here's why. Take my typical morning commute. The other day, I felt ambitious, getting up before dawn to work out during pre-business hours. I called an UberX. As always, when I matched for a ride, the driver's name and photo flashed on my screen. It was a forty-something black man driving a Prius. His photo showed a wide smile and beautifully coiffed dreadlocks.

My reaction to seeing a driver's photo is immediate. Each time, I have a knee-jerk reaction to their most basic demographic details. To be completely honest, I have a different reaction to Stephanie, the white, blond twenty-something on my screen versus Jian, the fifty-something Chinese man coming to pick me up. This is where Uber starts to work its magic. My human biases, typically lurking beneath the surface, come to awareness with the flash of the app.

Although I am embarrassed by these initial reactions, the last few months of studying unconscious bias have helped put this in perspective. Neuroscience proves that acting with bias doesn't make us bad people. It just makes us human. Given the variety and richness of our experiences, it is impossible for our brains to process all the information we receive. Instead, we process only a fraction of this information consciously, while allowing our unconscious brain to sort through the rest with the help of pattern-recognition. These patterns come from our personal experience and broader societal context (both good and bad). This approach can be helpful; we are able to quickly distinguish a butterfly from a bee and act accordingly. Unfortunately, this approach can also be harmful. When making decisions about human beings, for example, we automatically make assumptions about people, my collection of Uber drivers included. We apply implicit stereotypes according to race, gender, weight, age, and innumerable other dimensions. We're biased against those who look different from us, and even, in some cases, against those who look like us. Thus, when the face pops up on my app, it brings awareness to my crazy web of biases.

But here is the second thing about Uber. I am not limited to living within my biased assumptions about these people. Instead, as we zip across the city, I get to spend a perfectly orchestrated five, ten, or twenty minutes getting to know the person beyond the assumptions. It is the perfect set-up: a complete stranger, a delimited amount of time, and, if I'm lucky, a willingness to talk. It is my opportunity to connect across differences and prove to myself just how wrong my biases are. In the course of everyday life, it is an opportunity that you can find nearly nowhere else.

After calling an Uber the other day, I rode with a forty-something Middle Eastern man named

Muhammad. Had I jumped in a taxi with him, I would have kept to myself, falling in line with the norm of silence and ticking through emails on my phone. I would have left that car the same as I entered it. Instead, I met him as a human being. I asked him opening questions that went deeper and deeper. How long was he driving today? What did he do when he wasn't driving? What was important about that? I found that Muhammad spends his days as a stay-at-home dad. He loves to play bongos on the beach while his daughter dances. In addition, he planned to take his kids out to their favorite Neapolitan pizza place for dinner that night. I left the car after looking at pictures of his family and an enthusiastic mutual handshake.

I'm grateful to all my drivers for connecting across humanity, teaching me about their lives, and reprogramming my biases. I'm grateful to the traditionally dressed African man who gave me lessons on veganism. I'm grateful to the gay Palestinian who reminded me how accepting the Bay Area can be. I'm grateful to the overweight suburban dad who gave me a recipe for broccoli casserole. And, yes, I'm grateful to Uber.

What biases get in your way of seeing clearly?
When are these biases most triggered?

What helps you to see and navigate
around your biases?

How can you create opportunities to connect with
those different from you?

AWARENESS OF NORMS

This essay was originally published as the third in a trio of essays reflecting upon my engagement to my wife. As a lesbian couple, we had a clear opportunity to rewrite the script on the cultural norms associated with engagements. Yet, our story is an example of how anyone, through greater awareness and subsequent choice, can decide how to navigate norms.

AUGUST 10, 2014
SAN FRANCISCO, CALIFORNIA

In a same-sex relationship, there's not an option of falling back on traditional gender roles. Who cooks and who does the dishes? Who does the laundry and who mows the lawn? And more to the point (you see where I'm going with this), who proposes?

Recently, my girlfriend, Liz, surprised me by proposing (and I said yes). Then, a few weeks later, on a sunny Saturday in Napa, I proposed back to her. (Spoiler alert: She said yes too.)

The idea to counter-propose to my fiancée crystallized in the midst of my post-engagement glow. As I chatted with a friend over lunch, she shared how she and her wife always knew they would both propose, one to the other. Their choice was not who would propose, but instead who would go first.

I loved the mutuality of this. When Liz proposed, I was already noodling on the idea of proposing to her in the fall. In fact, I felt a little scooped when she asked me first. To be clear, I felt 99% excitement and 1% mild annoyance at being beaten to the punch by my clever, clever fiancée. Happily, though, this new mutual proposal idea meant that I could ask right back. We could both be the one summoning the courage to extend the question and the one thoughtfully answering, although perhaps with a higher degree of confidence the second time around.

My planning began with the symbol of my proposal. While Liz nailed my preferences by guessing I would want a traditional ring, I hadn't seen Liz be too enthusiastic about one. Every time I pushed or prodded on the ring idea, she didn't give me a clear answer. Separate from the ring, however, I had heard Liz talk about wanting a pocket watch for a very long time. So, I took off to a fine San Franciscan haberdasher and secured a beautiful 1902 Waltham pocket watch with an engraving of a trolley car on the back.

Next stop was the jeweler. Like Liz before me, I suffered upturned noses, exorbitant prices, and long lead times at every Union Square jeweler before returning to the same, sweet little shop where Liz designed my engagement ring. They engraved a lovely message on the inside of the watch and tuned it right up. When returning the finished product, the engraver even volunteered that this watch was very lucky indeed, citing the fact that the serial number (238) was the number of years from the country's founding to today (2014 minus 1776). Now, I wouldn't have thought of or celebrated that myself, but given Liz's patriotic history in the military, it seemed like a good omen.

After getting the go-ahead from every member of Liz's family, I pulled together the detailed plan. Liz's best friend from graduate school generously gave us wine tastings and engagement photos in wine country as our engagement gift; I would now enlist her as my accomplice. She agreed to position us for engagement pictures such that I would sit near Liz's feet and could easily shift into the traditional proposal posture. We schemed that we would start our day at a champagne house, where we could toast the proposal after Liz accepted (fingers crossed). I even assigned code words to coordinate in the moment. "That looks like a place for *pretty pictures*" was code for "We should probably do the proposal *over there*." "I need to reapply my *lipstick*" was code for "This is happening. I'm going to get my *purse with the pocket watch inside."*

When I finally turned to ask, I don't much remember what came out of my mouth. You think I would have been a bit more stable, considering my odds on the answer, but, in Liz's words, I "shook like a little leaf." By the time I popped open the pocket watch and hazily got through my lines, however, Liz said yes. Then champagne. And crying. And more crying.

There was something really special about asking Liz to marry me. I got to engineer a memorable, romantic moment for Liz, the Champion of the World at engineering memorable, romantic moments. She got to be surprised, a rarity for that observant lady. And together, we reaffirmed the mutuality of our relationship, wherein both of us can take the lead, and both of us can be wooed.

Interestingly, in the wake of both of our proposals, I heard all sorts of stories of other couples, both same-sex and heterosexual, being similarly intentional about their proposals. A female colleague proposed to her long-time boyfriend, citing that he had always been readier to get hitched, and she wanted to give a clear sign that she was ready too. A male friend initially rejected the idea of proposing (with its associated plotting and secret-keeping), but got on board when his girlfriend valued the traditional approach.

In our relationship, the answer to "who does what" has to be intentional, and it will continue to be so. I am grateful every day that we consciously choose the path that works best for us, beginning with our two unexpected proposals.

Where do you follow the script you've been given?

Where do you throw out the script and write a new approach yourself?

How is this the same or different when you are in relationship with someone?

AWARENESS OF
EXTERNAL PRESSURES

We are constantly "should-ing" on ourselves. Consciously or unconsciously, many of us experience a constant inner critique of what we should do, think, and act. Bringing consciousness to the external pressures in our lives allows us to intentionally navigate which of those things are in our service and which are just the echoes of other peoples' opinions knocking around in our heads.

AUGUST 25, 2014
SAN FRANCISCO, CALIFORNIA

My fiancée and I decided upon a wedding venue and are now moving on to tackle the specifics of bridal parties, videographers, and caterers. In doing so, I've realized anew how stepping into the role of bride-to-be brings with it all sorts of expectations.

Happily, at the same time, I've also realized how elegantly most brides navigate all these expectations. Weddings are just such extraordinary events that they jostle all of us out of our automatic, everyday routines and into a more intentional place. While the shoulds that we feel in the wedding-planning process are amplified over those of daily life, so is the intentionality with which your average bride faces these expectations.

IN ONE CORNER: THE SHOULDS

Sure, there is generally accepted flexibility within the guidelines, but everyone comes to the table with some longer or shorter set of expectations around weddings. For a bride planning a secular American wedding, the short version of this reads something like:

- You should have some sort of ceremony, religious or civil, that will proclaim you legally married
- You should tell everyone where to come and what to wear
- You should wear a dress
- You should wear white
- You should ask your best friends and family (particularly those of your gender) to show up in some sort of matching outfit
- You should decorate the location with more flowers than you've ever bought before
- You should feed everyone a meal (preferably with lots of accompanying alcohol)

- You should have a cake. In fact, you should make a big deal out of cutting it and then shove it in your spouse's face
- You should have dancing. And good music. Really good music.
- Some combination of your save the dates, wedding invitations, programs, and signage should be in coordinating designs
- You should pick colors to synchronize the look of the event
- You should document everything in extreme detail
- And, you should pick a convenient weekend day for all of this to happen

Why all the shoulds? To some extent, this is all incredibly useful. Expectations and norms like these help to write the cultural scripts that signal our change in marital status to the world. They help everyone understand that, yes, this event is, in fact, a wedding and give basic guidance on how everyone should act. They give us all parts to play without having to think about it a lot.

Beyond the cultural cues, many shoulds are our collective cultural wisdom around how to marry. They and the hundreds of other shoulds listed in bridal blogs, magazines, and books serve as a helpful mix of best practices of party-planning, smart aesthetic choices, and guidance from tradition. In so many ways, it's nice not to have to start from a blank slate.

But, it's also freeing to realize that none of the shoulds are necessary.

IN THE OTHER CORNER: INTENTIONALITY

My fiancée and I are not revolutionaries looking to defy every wedding tradition. In fact, I think we're both inclined to be more traditional rather than less. But we, like every other couple planning their wedding, have a choice. We can walk into the wedding-planning process and let ourselves be pummeled by all these shoulds. Or, we can be intentional about the event we create.

We can begin by identifying the shoulds and sorting them out from our true wants and needs. As we identify each should, we can also figure out where it comes from. Are they the voices of brides of eras past? The comments of our friends while debriefing wedding season? Our perception of what it takes to keep up with the Joneses? We can consider which of these expectations fit our aspirations and which ones don't serve us at all.

Being intentional means that we're not going to accept the template of a wedding. We're going to start from the beginning, with the *purpose* of this whole ritual and the *values* that we want it to express. We're going to build our wedding from there, adopting many of the shoulds that match with our own desires and throwing away the others.

The process isn't easy. It takes far more mental exertion to plan the wedding we want rather than accept each expectation. But so many weddings I've been to lately have shown exactly this intentionality, this willingness to make choices that are aligned with what the couple wants to create rather than thoughtlessly proceeding according to plan. Just this summer, I've watched a bride and groom rip up the dance floor with a professionally choreographed ballroom number, and I've been to multiple weddings with no dancing at all. I've been to by-the-book Christian and Jewish weddings, and I've listened to multiple (yes, multiple) Hindu/Christian fusion liturgies. I've taken a boat to a restaurant reception and wandered up a hill to eat in a barn. I've seen a wedding cake in the form of a tree stump and another surrounded by cardboard cutouts of sheep. I've traveled to hill stations, grooms' hometowns, and Hawaii. I've danced and hooted while the groom rapped about his love and clapped politely after the father-of-the-bride's speech. In so many ways, people are choosing the approach that fits the couple's personality, including where they want to invest, where they want to disinvest, and how they want people to feel.

However we act in our daily lives, the exceptionality of a wedding forces us to be intentional about how we design it. Now, the challenge is ours to sort through the shoulds and align on our ambition. I only hope we can do as well as our friends have done.

What recent experience did you feel had many shoulds associated with it?

What shoulds did you feel subject to?

How did you parse between the shoulds you accepted and the shoulds you discarded?

AWARENESS OF FEARS

I end this chapter with an essay on fears. More than any other dimension of our internal landscape, fears are the most powerful driver to see clearly and manage consciously. In doing so, we diffuse their power over us. If you take nothing else from this book, I hope that you leave with a greater ability to be present to your fears.

JULY 17, 2014
SAN FRANCISCO, CALIFORNIA

This past weekend I was lucky enough to catch up with a good friend who lives on the other side of the world. He mentioned that a friend of his was afraid of many things. Afraid of things happening. Afraid of things not happening. Afraid of being liked. Afraid of not being liked.

When my boyfriend passed away unexpectedly in 2010, I found myself afraid of nearly everything. I was afraid of never falling in love again, afraid I would fall in love again, afraid I would fall in love and then that person would pass away, afraid I would forget him, afraid I would always remember him, afraid of being judged for grieving in my own way, afraid that what I felt was real, afraid that what I felt was false. The list went on for pages in my journal.

Writing down the list of fears helped immensely. I found that the first step in moving through the fear was simply naming it. Give it form and substance. Put words to it. I didn't worry about the why behind it. Tracing each fear back to its psychological source wasn't the point. The point was getting rid of the fears. And, in order to do that, I needed to know what they were.

My list of fears was very long.

Then, I had to face them. By facing, I do not mean doing the thing you're afraid of or overcoming it in some forceful way (e.g., intercontinental flights for those afraid of flying). Instead, by facing, I mean just that: turning my face toward the fear. The point was to look at each fear instead of hiding from it. I needed to see them. Moreover, I needed to accept they existed.

So, for each fear, I just said "yes" to it. This was not a "yes" that I wished the fear would materialize, but instead an acknowledgment of its possibility. "Yes, I might end up alone." "Yes, people may judge me." "Yes, I might never be able to move past this." I just said yes. Yes, yes, yes, yes, yes, yes, yes. Yes, that might happen. Yes, this might happen. Yes, yes, yes. I said yes. I cried yes. I kept going with yes until there was nothing left.

And soon, I moved to a place of: "Okay. Yes. But, so what? So, what if it does happen? If that's what's going to happen, then I'll deal with it." And at that point the yes turned into a sort of acceptance of possibilities.

What I realized was that before I found yes, I was living in no. I was running from every fear. I was doing whatever I could to escape them. Trying every tactic. I was exhausted.

When I stopped running, I turned to face my fear. I always thought that once the fear caught me, I would be destroyed. Instead, when I stopped and let it catch up with me, it evaporated, ghost-like. It's almost like my fear passed straight through me.

When I started saying yes to fear, I also saw that the thing I feared and the fear itself were distinct. If the feared thing happened, whatever it was, I could deal with it. Step-by-step, I would figure it out, because that's what humans do. There was no use in being afraid of it. Why work myself up emotionally for a possible situation in the future? Saying yes allowed me to let this go instead of ducking, dodging, hiding, and running to avoid it.

My mental image of running from and then facing fear is that of Bugs Bunny. He runs away from Yosemite Sam, that creepy monster, or some other cartoon villain with all his might. But what actually diffuses the situation is stopping and facing the bugaboo. Stopping and facing lets us see that the villain, the fear, is laughable and inept.

If you are looking to let go of fear (or simply anxiety or nervousness), you can take the same approach.

- Make a long list of the things you're afraid of. It can be anything. Fear of things happening, fear of things not happening, fear of the judgment of others, fear of how you'll perceive yourself. Keep writing until you have no more fears to share. ("I am afraid of not having enough money," "I am afraid of my kids not going to the right school," "I am afraid if I speak up, people will think I'm too assertive," "I am afraid that if I don't go to PTA meetings, people will think I'm a bad parent." Whatever it is.)
- Go through the list. Say yes to each one. Keep on saying yes until the fear loses its magnitude
- When you're feeling afraid again, come back to the list or repeat the exercise anew. Write down your fears, say yes to each one, and let them go

The Fear Monster

What are you afraid of?

How do those fears drive you?

What happens when you say yes to the fears?

This brings us to the end of Chapter One, *Awareness*. In each essay, I examined a different unseen driver of behavior. Together, we have examined what it means to bring these drivers to more conscious awareness and to give us the possibility of making more intentional choices about them. Reflecting back on this chapter, I have three final questions:

What have you learned?

How are you different?

What else are you curious about?

CHAPTER TWO
REFLECTION

Reflection is a powerful tool—one that is central to answering the intentional question of *What do I want?* You may think that this question is best answered by simply sitting down, thinking hard enough, and coming up with an answer. In reality, navel-gazing only gets you so far. Often, it is more fruitful to reverse the approach by first living your life and then reflecting upon your lived experiences to extract the insights. Though the approach may seem inverted, understanding what you are doing often gives you a better sense of what you want.

This chapter is a collection of essays that provide embodied examples of that reflection. In these stories, you'll get to meet me more intimately than in any other section. Each essay typically begins with a situation—something as simple as playing with my daughter, cooking dinner, or having a conversation—which prompts examination of both the situation and myself. I hope that seeing the world through my perspective helps you to see more clearly what it looks like from yours. In addition, I want the process of reflection itself to become clearer and more accessible to you.

This is the chapter in which the questions following each essay become central. Do not miss the opportunity to step back, reflect, and build your self-knowledge.

REFLECTION ON COOKING

Lived experience is the best—the most frequent, the most tangible, the most tractable—prompt for reflection. Often, we learn more about ourselves by examining what we see ourselves tangibly doing instead of abstractly philosophizing. In this essay, even the act of cooking is a reason to reflect upon my values.

JANUARY 25, 2015
SAN FRANCISCO, CALIFORNIA

I spend a lot of my time thinking and writing about intentionality, this idea of mindfully and choicefully directing one's life. The thinking goes something like this: Our thoughts and our actions—and indeed our entire impact on the world—reflect our underlying beliefs and values, both conscious and unconscious. Yet, many people (myself included) do not always bring mindful awareness and conscious choice to these things.

While I celebrate the idea of intentionality, I (like everyone) can still be completely caught off-guard by the ways I unconsciously act, and the values those actions reflect. This week I surprised myself again. My realization?

I am way more frugal than I ever knew.

Case in point is the first twelve hours home after returning from this week's work trip to London. I came home, caught up with Liz, spent time with the puppy, ate some Goat Hill pizza (our favorite local pizza joint), and then…started sorting through the refrigerator. It's not that I was particularly hungry or even particularly bored and looking for something to do. Instead, I knew that there was a lot of food in the house when I left, and I wanted to make sure we weren't letting it go to waste.

To Liz's credit, she is easily as frugal as I am. Once, when in charge of organizing date night, Liz signed us up for a class on running a "zero-waste kitchen." They taught pickling extra vegetables, cheese-making to address your nearly expired milk, and broth-making for everything else. Whereas others may have thought this would be a strange romantic interlude, I absolutely loved it. We even got to make our own sauerkraut.

This past week, she focused on eating up leftovers from last week's camping adventure and working through the freezer. So, there wasn't much to do. Nonetheless, I pulled out my favorite frugality enabler: our new dehydrator.

It's not yet twenty-four hours later and my dehydrating adventures have been prolific. Leftover camping potatoes turned into crunchy parmesan potato bites. Previously pickled okra, jalapenos, and leftover corn became "Liz Mix." And more is on the way: peppers and garlic, mushrooms, jalapenos, carrots, and Brussels sprouts.

Despite all the time I spend thinking about how I want to consciously embody my chosen values, every so often something creeps up on me. This fit of kitchen management proves exactly that. Surveying my piles of dehydrated food, I thought, *Wow, this whole thing has made me really happy. I am way more frugal than I ever thought. And I embody that without really ever thinking about it.*"

I'll be reflecting about the values I live while munching on my potato bites.

When have you been surprised to find yourself acting in a certain way?

What did you learn about yourself?

What do your actions tell you about your values?

REFLECTION ON CONVERSATION

How do you speak? What words do you choose? Though speech seems straightforward (We're just talking to each other, right?), the motives behind our words can be complex—and revealing.

AUGUST 9, 2015
SAN RAFAEL, CALIFORNIA

I had lunch with a colleague this week during which we talked about her near-term plans and long-term aspirations over a bowl of bi bim bap. She reflected on options ranging from graduate school to life-long ambitions, from alternative career paths to renegotiating her relationship with her childhood pastimes. At the end of the discussion, as I munched on the leftover bowls of banchan, she paused, reflected for a moment, and remarked, "You ask really good questions."

I ask good questions? That's interesting, because I wasn't trying to ask good questions.

There was a time when I tried to ask good questions. In fact, I've wanted to ask good questions most of my life. As far back as elementary school, I sought to ask the interesting, non-obvious question to the teacher, less because I wanted to know the answer and more because I hoped to signal just how advanced my comprehension was. "I understand graphing real and imaginary numbers on a two-by-two, but what if you add a third dimension?" I delighted in stumping the teacher and didn't mind taking the class completely off-track. The goal of my question was not to understand, but to show how smart I was.

This inclination continued into the working world. Asking the right "high-gain question" was celebrated as a great skill. If someone was evaluating many options, I might say "It seems like there are really two approaches here: A or B. Which seems most useful to you?" Similarly, if someone was trying to understand a situation, I might say "In my experience, it is always a matter of X or Y. Which is at stake here?" My questions were crawling with clever frameworks and embedded advice. I casually showcased how brilliant I could be while simultaneously seeming helpful. While my questions presumed to help the other person find their direction, let's be honest: They were all about me.

As I've started to work on my ego (only partially successful to date), I've tried to stop asking questions for my own benefit and shift to asking questions in the service of others. This has prompted me to realize two things.

First, the smarter you try to be, the less useful you become.

Second, the most powerful questions are often the simplest.

Many have heard the perennial advice, "Ask open-ended questions." Beyond this, I propose adding the guidance, "Ask simple questions." It's not about providing a maze of options, a clever trade-off, or a new framing. It's not about leading people in the direction that you see unfolding. It is certainly not about receiving recognition for your endlessly clever perspective. Instead, it's about proposing the simplest question in service of the individual:

"What do you want?"

"What's important about that?"

"How do you feel?"

"How can I help?"

"What's next?"

Though I can't always get out of my own way, I am always most useful to others when I'm not trying to be clever. In other words, keep it simple, smarty.

What does the way you speak
tell you about yourself?

What image are you trying to portray through
the way you speak? Are you doing this
consciously or unconsciously?

How can you bring more intention to
the way you speak?

REFLECTION ON WORK

A core tenet of intentionality is that how we spend our time today is reflective of not only who we have been and the choices we have made, but also of who we will be in the future. When assessing where and how we spend our time, there are few places that emerge as more important than work. I read somewhere that the average person spends more of their life working than they spend with their family, pursuing their hobbies, or hanging out with friends. Although I don't know whether that's technically true, it is certainly consistent with my experience. Work has always been a centerpiece of my life and an omnipresent prompt for my development. It brings up both narrow questions about productivity and time management as well as bigger questions about meaning and fulfillment. Although we may assume work is an environment outside of our control—a world in which we play by the rules of the company in order to succeed—doing so is a missed opportunity. We cannot become the accidental products of our organizational environments. If we are going to live intentionally, then we need to take on the challenge of figuring out what type of people we want to be and translating that into the type of professionals we want to be—in every workaday word and action.

OCTOBER 19, 2014
SAN FRANCISCO, CALIFORNIA

I've been thinking a lot lately about the role the work plays in our fulfillment as human beings. What are we pursuing in life? What are we pursuing at work? Where are those objectives aligned or out of sync? Further, what do we do with all that?

Because I'm quite happy in both work and life these days, I'm lucky to approach this topic from a positive perspective. I sat back and asked myself, *How does work contribute to my fulfillment?*

There are two ways that work helps me follow my broader purpose in life.

First, my work is aligned with my mission and sense of purpose. I believe that my work—in and of itself—allows me to accomplish part of what I aspire to do in my short human life. Because of this, I deeply care that it's successful. I see myself in the process and the outcomes. Further, I learn things that matter to me, and I improve skills that are important to me. Work itself is meaningful and purposeful. That fundamental *passion for my work* contributes strongly to my sense of fulfillment.

Second, not only am I fulfilled by work, but work leaves room for me to find fulfillment in other ways. True, I work hard. Sometimes I devote entire days to work and work alone, starting conference calls early and finishing slides late. Despite this, I find that over the long run, there's time and space for all parts of me to be fulfilled. In addition to work, there's room for family, friends, community, exercise, hobbies, life administration, fun, travel, sleep, recovery, and beingness. Perhaps every day does not have every element, but the balance works out over a not-insignificant period of time. The impact is that not only is work fulfilling when I'm doing it, but work allows me to find fulfillment outside the office as well. This *ability to lead a full life* is the second connection between my work and my fulfillment.

So, I leave you with a framework to contextualize all of this. Does work contribute to your fulfillment? Where do you find yourself in the framework below?

How passionate are you about your work?

To what extent does work leave you space
to lead a full life?

Does work ultimately contribute to
your fulfillment or detract from it?

Over time, all parts of me are full.

ABILITY TO LIVE A FULL LIFE

Over time, parts of me are missing.

SORT OF	YES!
"To be honest, I'm just punching the clock."	*"Everything is in harmony."*
NO	SORT OF
"I am considering leaving." OR *"I feel trapped to stay."*	*"It's all-consuming, but it's worthwhile."*

PASSION FOR YOUR WORK

It's just a job.

I absolutely love what I so.

© Whipple Callahan, 2014

Work and Fullfillment

REFLECTION ON WEDDINGS

There are few experiences I found as difficult to process as my wedding. The experience was so complex and multi-faceted that it took weeks of time—including both numerous conversations and plenty of journaling—to figure out what I learned from it. Sometimes the insights from our lived experiences are not obvious; it takes time, patience, and effort to understand what has happened and how that informs who we are becoming.

NOVEMBER 22, 2015
SAN FRANCISCO, CALIFORNIA

This weekend, I attended the fourth wedding since my own ceremony in August. With nearly three months of perspective and many more weddings under my belt, I'm finally ready to reflect back on what I learned through the entire wedding process.

Starting with the planning, *I'm grateful that we invested in what we cared about.* In the months leading up to the wedding, it horrified me to find out just how much work this whole affair can be. So, I'm glad we picked our battles. Since I cared a lot about the ceremony, we wrote every word of it ourselves. Since

Liz cared about the music, she picked every song by hand. The flowers that we didn't care about were perfectly serviceable and lovely accents to the event. I'm glad we reserved our energy and didn't worry about what mattered less to us.

My first realization during wedding week was that *we needed every moment available.* In addition to our wedding day, we held an entire week's worth of events: drinks at our favorite dive bar, biking across the Golden Gate Bridge, wine tasting in Sonoma, breakfasting with our families, picnicking with everyone in the Presidio, and celebrating our rehearsal at the restaurant where we had our first date. About 24 hours into our 100-plus-hour celebration, I saw how much I needed all the remaining time to connect with people and spend solid time with all of them (as well as Liz). Call me an extrovert, but I couldn't soak up enough. I'm grateful we had the luxury of time with so many guests.

In arranging the last-minute details for the wedding, I was touched by *how people made themselves of service in a beautiful way.* In addition to our families and our wedding parties (who all played wonderfully supportive roles), there were unexpected guests who jumped in to help. The uncles carried all the snacks for the wine bus. The former classmates helped transport all the alcohol after the picnic. The friend from business school diligently held my drink while I danced. None of them had formal roles, and yet all were so enthusiastically helpful. We will pay this support forward at every wedding we attend.

At the wedding itself, I found the old adage to be true: "If something can go wrong, it will go wrong." *Something will go wrong, and you need to let it go.* For us, the one thing that went wrong at our wedding was the coffee cups; they were paper cups instead of proper mugs. (Oh, the horror!) Did our guests notice? No. Did we notice? Yes. Did our guests care? No. Did we care? Less than we would have thought, but more than we should have. Let it go and enjoy all that is right.

Looking back at the wedding as a whole, *my favorite moments were completely unscripted*: the drive to the venue with my parents and a beloved bridesmaid, peering out the window as guests arrived, my instinctual reaction when I first saw Liz, the champagne pop, the end of my father's speech, the first song the DJ played, the last song the DJ played, and the plate of grilled cheese someone gave me late-night. Perhaps more than anything else, I loved the quiet of Liz and I taking the dog for a walk in the full moon well after the wedding was over. I'm glad there was room to savor the little moments.

Previously, I struggled to wrap my head around the whole event. However, since reflecting more, I've realized that *every part of a wedding is a public affair.* Not only do you celebrate your wedding in public, but you process it in public. Typically, I work through life events independently, journaling on my experiences. This approach didn't resonate for the wedding. It was only when I started to talk to people about the wedding—to hear about their experiences and share my own—that I started to see the meaning of the whole event more clearly. For all the relationship moments that are lived privately, a wedding is public. Meaning is created between people—between Liz and me, between us and our guests—and not in my head alone. Once I understood this, the debrief conversations with guests and my wife took on a new importance. Liz and I jumped into co-authoring a journal of our collective wedding week events to capture everything from a full perspective. We experienced it together, so we needed to process it together as well.

So, to conclude, thank you for digesting this with me and bringing yet another level to the public commitment Liz and I made in August. I'm grateful that you're all bearing witness to the journey.

What have you learned from the
milestones in your life?

How are you of service to others at
their peak moments in life?

What life experiences do you need help from
others to make sense of?

REFLECTION ON PREGNANCY

Sometimes we are prompted to reflect because we are facing the same situation for a second time. For example, the following essay was written while pregnant with baby number two. When sorting through pregnancy for a second time, I was able to see my role in it more clearly. The similarities and differences between the parallel experiences gave me clues as to what was consistent and inconsistent in myself over time. The second time around in any situation can help us see ourselves more clearly.

SEPTEMBER 3, 2018
NORWALK, CONNECTICUT

What has been most notable about this second pregnancy is how different it feels from the first.

The first time around, I prepared myself for what I anticipated would be the life-changing and spiritual experience of pregnancy and birth. My friend Moshe fed the fire, commenting on how spiritual it must be to have life growing within you and to be in such a powerfully creative place. I desperately wanted to feel that way.

That first time around I wanted to be fully prepared for parenthood. We took every single birth class. I mean every single one. Not just the birthing and breastfeeding and first-year parenting classes, but also the infant CPR/first aid classes and the infant massage classes. I even convinced Liz to come with me to a prenatal partners yoga workshop.

Working with the midwives, my birth preferences that first time were extensive. They articulated a plan for natural labor and reflected weeks of research on how things might go best. By the time I went into labor, I was ready in every way—spiritually, intellectually, logistically—to be transformed by this experience.

Thirty-hours of labor later, on August 2nd, 2016, Elliott joined us. The midwife said I looked surprised that there was a baby at the end of childbirth, and she was correct. So much of my preparation had focused on me, on my experience of birth, and what I would learn from all these things that I couldn't clearly see how this was the start of so much more.

There is so much which is different this time around, both in my circumstances and in myself. I wish I could say it's because I'm infinitely wiser, but instead I continue to learn from every new experience. Here is what I'm seeing this second time around:

It's Actually About the Baby. The most important difference between my pregnancies is that it has shifted between pregnancy being about me to pregnancy being about the baby. I know the punchline now; God-willing, childbirth ends in parenthood. The whole point is bringing this little man into the world in a safe and healthy way. So, instead of being curious about the experiences I'll have, I'm just excited to meet the little man. There's far less interest in "What am I like in this situation?" and more interest in "What's he going to be like?"

Who Has Time for That? I realistically don't have the time to be so self-centric this time around. I could point to a whole portfolio of demands on my time, but the ultimate cause is my daughter, Elliott. Two-year-olds do a remarkable job occupying every available minute of time, and I am (mostly) happy to give her those moments. As a result, pregnancy looks different. Last time around, I prioritized weekly acupuncture, gentle but diligent workouts, and frequent prenatal massages. This time, I sit in the closet while Elliott delights in opening and shutting the door, or we lie together on the floor, waiting for imaginary deer and lions to come visit.

I Know I Don't Have Control. Even if I don't always act as if it's true, I know through experience that I have nearly no control over all of this—from pregnancy to childbirth to parenting. The most important processes, physical and otherwise, unfold naturally. Although I still struggle to act in accordance with this insight, I realize I am less in a position of control and more in a position of surrender. No birth plan, only birth preferences. A recognition that birth will come when it comes and go how it goes. And, most important, no expectations that the lessons learned caring for Elliott as a baby will translate into any better ability to care for number two.

And so... Sometimes I step back and reflect on all this, wondering if my different emerging relationships to my two children, starting in even these early months of pregnancy, are simply the first manifestation of birth-order conditioning. Though still in utero, Elliott had attention and focus throughout my pregnancy. She's maintained much of that while this little man has developed inside me. For his part, the little man has either enjoyed or suffered through a pregnancy with far less of a maniacal focus on him. At times, I've blamed myself that I have not been more pregnancy-focused, but my wise friend, Nema, advised me, "The baby will make sure he draws in what he needs."

Little Man, I hope you have everything you need. We can't wait to meet you.

What are you currently facing again
(for a second or third time)?

How is the situation different from the first time?

How is your response different?
What are you learning about yourself
from the differences?

REFLECTION ON MOVING

Some life choices have an outsized impact on your evolution as a person, and moving strikes me as one of those. In relocating yourself from one place to another, you have the opportunity to intentionally remake yourself along nearly every dimension. You also have the opportunity to reflect critically upon the experience of moving itself to understand what it is giving you and what it is taking away.

OCTOBER 15, 2017

NORWALK, CONNECTICUT

The Callahan clan moved from California to Connecticut earlier this year. I wrote about that transition on *The Intentional* and posted it to the appropriate social media channels. Among the chorus of wisdom and encouraging words, there was no comment more apt than my friend Michael reminding me that, *"Qui transtulit sustinet."*

"Qui transtulit sustinet" or "He who transplanted sustains" is the state motto of Connecticut. I recalled the motto from the first time I transplanted myself to this state—from my hometown of Port Huron to college in New Haven. Now, here it was, cropping up again as I moved to Connecticut a second time.

There are a couple of meanings of the motto. The first implies that he who transplanted you will sustain you, indicating that God (who brought the settlers to America) would support them (in the new land). I prefer a second interpretation of the motto, however, the one that makes it more personal: He who transplants himself sustains.

The idea of transplanting oneself resonates with the advice, "You have to repot yourself every once in a while." The philosophy of repotting people is the same as repotting plants. When our growth slows or stops, it's time to move. We pull ourselves up by the roots, shake off the dirt, and settle into a new pot with fresh soil. The pot should be a bit bigger than the old but not overly big. We need space to grow without being overwhelmed.

Although the goal of repotting is growth, when plants are first moved, they often enter a period of shock. Similarly, instead of thriving, we appear wilted and thirsty as we adjust to our new circumstances. Change, as everyone knows, is hard. That said, over time, the new pot, with more space and refreshed nutrients, enables the new growth and, eventually, new bloom.

While repotting sounds wise, it is often painful and unpleasant. Your pot may be so comfortable that you could stayed there forever. Yet, if we're committed to growth, we must repot ourselves instead of waiting for some cosmic gardener to change our circumstances. As John Gardner wrote in *Self-Renewal*, only by intentionally repotting can we grow into our fullness as humans. He wrote:

> "Most of us have potentialities that have never been developed simply because the circumstances of our lives never called them forth. Exploration of the full range of our own potentialities is not something that we can safely leave to the chances of life. It is something to be pursued systematically, or at least avidly, to the end of our days. We should look forward to an endless and unpredictable dialogue between our potentialities and the claims of life—*not only the claims we encounter but the claims we invent.* And by the potentialities I mean not just skills, but the full range capacities for sensing, wondering, learning, understanding, loving, and aspiring."

When we made the decision to move across the country, it was not pleasant. We didn't happily repot.

Instead, we felt our roots clinging to the California soil with all our might. Yet, when the opportunity called to investigate our new potentialities—to see what new growth might be possible—we took it. So, we find ourselves here, repotted in Connecticut. We are certainly still adjusting from the initial shock, but we hope that the family who transplanted will not only sustain, but grow in an even bigger way.

When have you re-potted yourself?

What did you learn from that transition?

Are you due to be re-potted again soon?
How might you re-pot without actually moving?

REFLECTION ON MOTIVATIONS

This essay is less tethered to lived experience and more conceptual in nature. That said, it provides yet another model of what reflection can look like. Sometimes we do think abstractly about life, and those reflections are also instructive.

MARCH 30, 2015
DENVER, COLORADO

I've been thinking a lot about why. Why, why, why?

In school, we were taught to ask the five W's (and the accompanying H) to dissect situations in literature and beyond: "Who? What? Where? When? Why? How?" It trips off the tongue so elegantly that it almost runs together into one word, the all-encompassing "Whowhatwherewhenwhyhow?" The list seems comprehensive and complete, as if there are no other questions to ask.

Of that list of fundamental questions, the why has wandered into the forefront over the past few decades. Modern management theory, as articulated in the Toyota Production System, teaches us to ask why at least five times to get to the root cause of a problem.

Similarly, Simon Sinek, author of Start with Why, claims that the soul of an organization is not the how or the what, but instead the why behind its actions.

I love the why. I resonate with the why. I am a big supporter of the why.

Still, there's a problem with why. Our current usage of why is so broad that it's confusing. "Why?" can be answered on many levels. A legitimate answer to, "Why did you spend Saturday with your family?" can be anything from, "Because my kids had a soccer game," to "Because I prioritize my family and put them first." To use the examples above, the why behind root-cause analysis and the why that Simon Sinek preaches are actually quite distinct.

There are (at least) two whys in the world: The first why is *the proximal why*. It is the immediate impetus for an event or action and is often more of a superficial answer.

"Why did you have a sandwich for lunch?" "Because that's what I brought from home."

"Why are we changing our branding and messaging?" "Because the boss said so."

"Why do you work at this company?" "Because they pay me."

The second why is *the underlying why*. You can think of this as the big why. Instead of stopping with immediate causality, the underlying why invokes our purpose, values, and aspirations.

"Why did you have a sandwich for lunch?" "Because I pack my lunch every day to save money and eat better."

"Why are we changing our branding and messaging?" "Because we want to make clear our mission of delivering exceptional customer service in each interaction people have with our company."

"Why do you work at this company?" "Because I'm able to help source ingredients responsibly for packaged foods and impact the health of people around the world."

If we keep on asking ourselves the "Whowhatwherewhenwhyhow?" litany, we tend to gravitate toward the proximal why and forego the underlying why. Because the English language currently conflates the two whys, we have difficulty answering both in a clear and satisfactory way. I propose separating the whys and adopting new taxonomy.

Let's allow the proximal why to keep the word why. It's common, it's easy, and it's established. Then, let's introduce a new word for the underlying why. Let's give it a separate identity so it becomes its own distinct and important question. We could call it anything really: "Whereto?" "What to?" "Toward?" "Pineapple upside-down cake?" For simplicity, though, let's try wherefore.

The etymology of wherefore makes it a good fit for the underlying why. It is an archaic form of why also defined to mean "for what" or "for what reason." Perhaps the most famous use of wherefore is from Juliet's soliloquy about Romeo in which she asks, "Wherefore art thou Romeo?" (i.e., "Why are you Romeo?") This question invites deep reflection. It is not sufficiently answered by, "He is Romeo because that's what his parents named him," but instead calls forth questions of the meaning of names, the importance of family affiliation, and the function of fate.

PROXIMAL WHY	UNDERLYING WHY
"Why?"	*"Wherefore?"* *(or alternative)*
• Focuses on immediate causality	• Points to bigger purpose, values, and aspirations
• Often superficial	• Often deeper
• Impersonal at times	• May be personal and revealing
• Passive and unconscious	• Active and conscious
The automatic focus of "why" questions today	An aspirational and necessary addition to the "why" discussion

© Whipple Callahan, 2015

The Two Whys

I invite you to start using "wherefore?" in your own life. Reflecting on my own decisions, when I'm able to clearly answer the wherefore, I've often been more intentional about my path. When I don't know the wherefore, I've been hasty, unreflective, or, frankly, just lazy.

It is a lovely (if aspirational) idea: that people would be asking themselves not only the easier why but the harder wherefore. With any luck, our children will be soon asking themselves exactly that at school. And then, the question will become: "Whowhatwherewhenwhyhowwherefore?"

In what situations do you know the underlying why behind your actions?

In what situations do you miss the underlying why?

What is your big wherefore in life?

REFLECTION ON PARENTING

Nothing invites me to reconsider my behaviors more than parenting. First, it invites me to be more present. Present to diaper changes. Present to toddler tantrums. Present to all sorts of experiences I'd rather skim over. Second, parenting invites me to abandon my expectations and loosen my sense of control. Nothing is as I expect it to be. Nothing is as I want it to be. Nothing is according to plan. But third and most important, parenting invites me to find the meaning in the small things. My friends call it the "liturgy of the ordinary," the way in which engaging consciously and intentionally in everyday life can transmute those experiences into something meaningful and even holy. With my kids, a hot dog lunch becomes momentous, a walk down the street becomes precious, and laundry becomes a home economics lesson. Little things are invested with bigger meaning. And, trust me, there are lots of little things to take care of.

OCTOBER 23, 2016
SAN FRANCISCO, CALIFORNIA

Since my daughter Elliott's birth, our friends and family have been deferential about how busy we must be. On some level, they're right. Frequently, there has barely been time to shower, eat, or walk the dog. But *busy* doesn't feel like the right word to describe these early weeks. Busy implies a long list of things to accomplish and not enough time. Indeed, if we were just living in a state of busy-ness, we could perhaps adjust by increasing our capacity or speeding things up.

After years in the workforce, so much of me thrives on busy-ness: its sense of buzzy productivity, the little checkmarks in boxes, and the haze of meaning that comes from simply getting stuff done. In many ways, I *wish* I could change all the diapers, pump all the milk, and share all my love by just working hard to do so. Mothering for today? Check, check, check.

On the contrary, with Elliott, there is nothing to check off the list; we feed, diaper, rock, and play with her over and over again. Yes, I have other non-baby items to accomplish. However, I long ago realized that days and weeks could go by with nothing getting checked off that list, even though I was constantly occupied. The to-do list of discrete, successive items has been replaced by endless, iterative tasks.

Through it all, I haven't felt a lack of time or a sense of hurry that being "busy" implies. Everything is done when it needs to be done, on Elliott's clock. I can't change ten diapers by noon to hit my quota and declare myself done for the day. There is plenty to do, but it's impossible to rush it. Similarly, it's impossible to run out of time to do what needs to be done.

In sum, it's less that I feel busy and more that I feel completely *consumed*. The reality of life with baby is that every moment is spent care-giving in the present. I am challenged to slow down and invest every act with big love. I am challenged to attend to whatever Elliott needs right now, without anticipation or distraction. I am challenged to be less busy and more present.

As she draws me more into mamahood, Elliott brings me more into the moment and more into myself.

Realistically, I still find myself trying to accomplish things according to my old habits; instead of nursing with full presence at two o'clock in the morning, I sometimes multi-task, teaching myself baby sign language or editing my new book. But I'm increasingly finding big meaning in letting myself be consumed by these everyday acts of childcare. And I love it.

What meaning do you find in everyday tasks?

Where could you benefit from being more present?

What would happen if you slowed down?

REFLECTION ON INTROSPECTION

I have noticed that reflection must be constant. We cannot reflect once, or even infrequently, and expect that will be sufficient. Reflection must be a discipline.

JULY 20, 2014
SAN FRANCISCO, CALIFORNIA

I was chatting with a minister-friend of mine the other day about one of the universal truths of self-reflection: Self-reflection has a short shelf life.

I've noticed this phenomenon in self-development workshops I've both attended and facilitated. You spend a few hours navel-gazing, journaling, or in a coaching conversation and come up with the most brilliant insights. "Who knew that my fear of spiders was what's holding me back from volunteering in the Amazon!" or "Wow, fear and love are opposites! I never thought of it that way!" The insights are always that: insightful. You see things you didn't see previously. You feel a burst of energy for attacking the world with your new understanding. With a bit of accountability, you use the power of your insight to push forward into an evolved way of being. It's the core of personal evolution.

The problem is that yesterday's insight is today's yawn-worthy platitude. Insights are so quickly absorbed into our current state of thinking that they're no longer insightful.

I notice this same phenomenon when I share my personal insights with others. Because others rarely have the same obstacles obscuring their sight, sharing a powerful personal realization is often met with "Yeah, you just realized that now?" It's not that the insight is silly or simple, but instead that it doesn't have the same resonance for someone else.

Although insights seem quite generic or obvious, their situational relevance is what makes them powerful. Insights are exactly what you need to realize—at this point in time, in this situation, for you and you alone. They're hard to share. Sometimes, they're hard to remember, and even if you did remember them, they wouldn't be as relevant a day, week, or month later.

All this leads to my conclusion: Self-reflection has a short shelf life.

As you look back at your big 'ah-ha' moments, which insights have been short-lived and which have persisted?

What is the lesson that you find yourself learning over and over again in different contexts?

What is the personal challenge that deserves your attention and reflection now?

This brings us to the end of Chapter Two, *Reflection*. In each essay, I looked back through a reflective lens at a different life event, unpacking the experience and searching for insight about myself and the world. As you close this chapter, I ask you to make a plan for how you will similarly reflect on your own lived experience as you move through life. Here's the exercise.

First, think back.

How have you approached reflection in the past?

What form does your reflection typically take (e.g., journaling, driving to work, meditating, going out for a run)?

How frequently do you do it?

How effective is your reflective approach at helping you come to insights?

What needs to be true (about you, about your circumstances) for you to find value in reflection?

And, very important,

**Do you intentionally make time and space
for reflection, or is it incidental?**

Now, look forward. I ask that you try taking a more intentional approach to your reflection. This need not be a life-long commitment. I am simply asking you to experiment with being intentional in your reflection and then seeing how that goes for you.

**What time and space do you want
to set aside for reflection?**

How frequently will you do it?

**What do you need to do to increase the odds of
being successful?**

**What do you need to do to hold
yourself accountable?**

Once you have articulated what you want your reflective practice to look like, go to your calendar. Schedule the next time you will sit down for conscious reflection. Start with a blank sheet of paper and the two intentional questions: *What do I want?* and *What am I doing?*

CHAPTER THREE
ALIGNMENT

As we've already discussed, the heart of intentionality is the alignment of *what you want* and *what you do*. This is the unglamorous, daily drudgery of intentionality. It is present in everything from choosing how to spend a Saturday (with your kids? working on your hobby? cleaning the house?) to selecting what you eat for lunch (organic apple? burger out with friends? sandwich alone at your desk?). Every moment is an opportunity to create who you are becoming.

You can achieve this alignment many ways. As illustrated in the simple examples above, you can choose *actions* that manifest your values. This is a relatively straightforward tactic. Second, you can adopt a *mindset* that reflects how you consciously want to approach the world. Though more abstract, this is also an intentional choice in which you align yourself—in this case, your way of thinking—to your ambitions. Third, you can create *meaning* through crafting actions which directly and explicitly reflect your values, typically by employing the mechanics of ritual. This chapter is divided into three sub-chapters discussing each of these movements toward alignment: through aligning actions, through choosing mindsets, and through creating meaning.

ALIGNING ACTIONS

Aligning *what you do* with *what you want* often begins by aligning your actions. Each action has the power to support or derail you in your evolution toward your envisioned state. It may seem strange to think that the tone of voice you use with your dog, your selection of an afternoon snack, or the way you drive to work has any substantial consequences. But, as I have articulated, your life—and moreover, your entire identity—is the sum of your choices. By this logic, yelling at your dog every day means you become a person who is mean to animals, eating a cookie every afternoon causes you to become overweight, and habitually driving too fast makes you a liability to others. In each situation, you can respond to the circumstances incidentally, or you can act intentionally in alignment with what you want to achieve. By consciously aligning actions you create yourself and your reality one moment at a time. This section tackles exactly that challenge through the lens of multiple everyday moments: while eating, dressing, shopping, organizing, and planning.

ALIGNING ACTIONS
WHILE EATING

While questions about what we eat may seem mundane, we are obsessed with them. The amount of time and energy we variously dedicate to nutrition, diets, fine dining, and home cooking points to how preprogrammed we are as humans to care about these things. Indeed, eating is one of the most personally transformative acts possible. We prepare food, ingest it into our bodies, and, in effect, allow that substance to become part of us. Ultimately, just as we cannot escape the need to eat, so we cannot escape the intimate relationship between the act of eating and the formation of our selves.

SEPTEMBER 29, 2014
SAN FRANCISCO, CALIFORNIA

Between dieting in preparation for my wedding and attempting to count calories, I've been thinking a lot about food. The point of my wedding diet was bringing consciousness to certain foods—dairy and sugar among them—and figuring out how I reacted to cutting out each one. As I've moved past that approach, I've started to think less narrowly (i.e., What happens when this one thing goes away?) and more broadly (i.e., What happens when I eat anything?). Physically, emotionally, and otherwise, what life do I create for myself as I ingest each bite?

A good friend told me, "Food is the place where we develop and exert our integrity." Integrity, in this case, could mean following through on our commitments, such as our ability to stick to a diet or maintain our veganism over time. On a broader scale, though, integrity in eating could also mean choosing food that reflects who we are and what we value. For example, at different times I value health, convenience, appearance, social connection, cultural experience, tradition, sustainability, and frugality when I decide what to eat. Not all of those values are reflected in this morning's espresso or my mid-day fried rice, but my choices are the more-or-less successful reflection of a constellation of values I strive to honor.

I am what I eat, from the molecules that make up my food, to the values my food reflects.

And you are too. You can imagine that we all eat from a veritable pu pu platter of values every day.

Yet, here's the thing about values. You can't honor all of them all the time. It's tough to find the afternoon snack that, at the same time, is frugal, is healthy, and communicates your sense of adventure.

So, we make trade-offs. We give up some things to accommodate others.

I know I won't always be the perfect reflection of my values, but my hope is that I can keep on consciously choosing what I eat. I've learned over the past months that I don't live better by excluding sugar or including dairy. I've learned that I eat best when I eat consciously—conscious of not only the basic gastronomical dimensions of what and how much I eat, but also the why and the how behind it.

And with that, I am finishing defrosting the ratatouille, the most tangible manifestation of my values of health, appearance, and frugality you'll see from me all day.

What values did you eat today?

What values did you trade off today?

What values do you aspire to eat?
What would it look like to eat in accordance
with them?

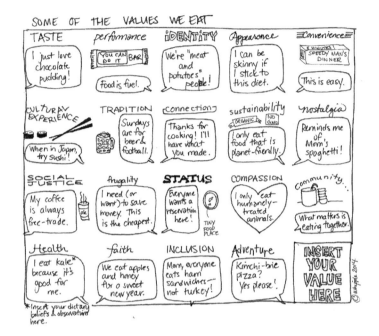

The Values You Eat

ALIGNING ACTIONS
WHILE DRESSING

Dressing and grooming are intimate forms of self-expression. Yet because we do them every day, it is easy to present ourselves in ways that we adopted long ago and don't actively consider. As you put on your pants, one leg at a time, it is powerful to reflect on whether you are making an intentional statement or an accidental one with your appearance. Dressing is an invitation everyday to align our visible exterior with our interior sense of self.

SEPTEMBER 6, 2017
NORWALK, CONNECTICUT

My wife and I were walking down the main drag in Westport the other day when we passed a group of high schoolers. We overheard the following:

"I have my first day outfit figured out, but I still need to buy my second- and third-day clothes."

I remember being a version of that high schooler (albeit, one who only planned for the first day). Specifically, I remember preparing for my first day of high school with care. My mom took me down to Jacobson's, the Detroit-area department store, to shop, and I put together the best outfit: light blue jeans with more-than-average flare, a yellow fitted sweater, and, the best part, a silver necklace with block letter beads spelling M-E-R-E-D-I-T-H.

On that first day of high school, I wanted to be perceived as stylish, grown-up, and popular. My first-day-of-school fashion efforts faltered quickly. I didn't have the second- and third-day outfits planned, nor did I find any joy in doing so. After all, I didn't value fashion. Like many teenagers, I only valued the approval it might provide if I crafted my image appropriately.

To my surprise, when I started my new job in April, I was no different from the ninth-grader in the wide pants that I used to be. I bought a new dress and blazer that struck the right balance of casual and professional. I got a reasonable haircut and even spent a minute considering whether I should wear make-up. Although I'm more comfortable with myself in important ways now, I could still see the instinct of approval-seeking playing out.

Opening a new school year and starting a new job are both entryways into new group formation. Our approval-seeking tendencies, which may be more or less activated in the day-to-day, are piqued by this newness. Uncertain about our status and situation, we bring reawakened questions of identity, inclusion, and approval. *If I show them who I really am, will I be included? Will the real me be a fit for this role?* And, more broadly *Who do I have to be for you to approve of me?*

Byron Katie, in her work on thoughts and approval, suggests considering each item you pick out and articulating:

"With this <item of clothing>, I want you to think that <perception of you>."

Or, alternatively,

"I am hiding this <part of self>, so you won't think that <perception of you>."

[From Byron Katie's I Need Your Love—Is that True?*]*

When is the last time you picked out your "first-day" outfit, designed your Burning Man costume, or dressed to make a particular impression? More important, what can those choices tell you about how you want others to perceive you? With clothing, we have a unique opportunity to look at something as tangible and seemingly inconsequential as our first-day clothes and get curious about what we can learn from our choices.

What do these seemingly mundane choices about
clothes tell you about yourself?

How do you use clothes to manage
your desired image?

If you don't manage your identity through
your clothes, how do you convey who you are?

ALIGNING ACTIONS
WHILE SHOPPING

In a world in which resources are becoming more and more scarce, becoming a conscious consumer has impact, not only on you, but on our planet as well. Intentionality as a consumer—or the lack thereof—has wide-reaching and long-lasting consequences.

JANUARY 5, 2017
INDIANOLA, IOWA

Over the holidays, I joined the extended family in a trip to the Jordan Creek Mall outside of Des Moines. The excursion was primarily designed to eat some famous local burgers, allow the kids to let off some steam, and stretch our legs. What I didn't expect were many bigger reflections on consumerism.

My mall-going days were concentrated in my youth and, to this day, retain a haze of teenage uncertainty and discomfort. Pop culture told me that, as a teenage girl, I was supposed to count shopping as a pastime. *Shop 'Til You Drop* was a beloved after-school game show for my brother and me. The Mall Madness board game was a particular favorite among my peers.

For the entire decade of the 1990s, the mall was simply the cool place to hang out. For me, however, anytime I went to the mall (or shopping more broadly), I felt like I was self-consciously playing a role. Wasn't I having fun buying earrings at Claire's? Didn't I love trying on clothes all day and finding just *the perfect thing*? Wasn't it great to arrive without any particular plan, but to treat yourself to something you didn't even know you wanted? I know many people enjoy shopping, but it was never fun for me, and I was in my twenties before I could figure that out.

As I've grown up, I've designed a very different relationship with shopping. Liz and I live an Amazon-enabled life. We assess and agree upon our need before buying each item. We research the best offering in each category, whether through a quick spot-check of Amazon reviews or more extensive online diligence. We are quick to return items that don't satisfy our needs, packing them up and shipping them back. In short, there's no such thing as an impulse purchase. The process is all overarchingly intentional.

These narrow online shopping habits don't expose us to the breadth of American consumerism. This is why my mall visit this holiday season was so surprising; it popped my Amazon shopping bubble and exposed me to the broader landscape of consumerism. Here are a few observations from my mall wanderings.

First, I was struck by the sheer volume of items for sale: iPhone cases, laser-cut cat images, Christmas ornaments, clothes, clothes, clothes! So many things! Who would buy all this? Where did it come from? Who made it all? And where would it all go after it was used and loved? The volume of merchandise for sale made me think about the lives of these items before these shelves (the raw materials, the producers, their working conditions) and their existence after these shelves (the joy or utility these items might bring, the landfills and recycling centers where they might go). Receiving my single, intentionally purchased item in a box on my doorstep focuses me on this sole item and my use alone. Walking through the mall reminded me of the broader life cycle of this vast array of goods.

Further, in the intra-holiday period, I was struck by the dominance of the deal. Nearly every store had a sale: 65% off! Buy one, get one! Everything $1! I could viscerally feel their allure, and I too wanted to stock up on $3 Bath and Body Works soaps and $1 turtlenecks. Thus, while I typically buy what I need with intention, my mall trip reminded me of how frequently we buy items on impulse. It's crazy: even when we're trying hard to be thoughtful, it's difficult to say no to an experience designed to maximize spending, regardless of need.

To be clear, living in the online shopping bubble does not make me immune to the negative sides of consumerism. For every pair of jeans I buy online, there's still an immense amount of textile waste generated, and I'm certainly guilty of collecting a pile of cardboard boxes nearly every week. Yet, my mall trip prompted me to reflect on the aspects of consumerism often hidden to us online shoppers—and to recommit to how I want to buy items. In the face of all these things to buy, I want to purchase only high-quality items with responsible sourcing and a long, usable life. In the face of impulse buys, I want to be even more thoughtful about purchasing only the few vital items we need.

What do your shopping habits tell you about what you value?

What are the consequences—for you, for others, for the environment—of the way you shop?

How might you shop with more intention?

ALIGNING ACTIONS
WHILE ORGANIZING

Under the superficial veneer of possessions is an invitation to profound meaning. Our possessions—everything from second-hand electronics to mega-yachts—are extensions of ourselves. They are the outward manifestations of our most closely held values. What does it mean to acquire? To possess? To consume? To display? To dispose? What do these decisions say about who we are? Through the lens of intentionality, how do our decisions about our possessions not only change us, but create us?

DECEMBER 21, 2018
PLAYA HERMOSA, COSTA RICA

One of the themes of the last few months has been stuff—the physical items with which we surround ourselves. The addition of my son in September prompted a flurry of preparations and reconsideration of all our possessions. We started by sorting through all our baby gear. Soon enough, we found ourselves shuffling our lesser-used Christmas ornaments and fancy china off to a new storage room. I spent my evenings sorting through memory boxes from my childhood and sending boxes of photos off to be digitized. Now, even though we're traveling for two months and away from most of our possessions, we still spend a fair amount of time schlepping suitcases from one location to another, packing and unpacking the things we brought, and organizing our items into new spaces to be functional.

All of this stuff management has made me reflect upon how we manage our things. Long ago, when Liz and I moved in together, we agreed upon a number of guiding principles about how we would manage our combined stuff. It was less guidance that we aspired to but more an articulation of our already-shared philosophy. It included such guiding principles as the following.

One in/one out. The concept is simple: buy a sweater, get rid of a sweater. The challenge here is that you need to accurately baseline what you own at the start. This ensures you are not adhering to the letter of the law and unintentionally maintaining a bloated pants collection or never letting yourself buy the extra set of socks you need to make it through the week. However, if you follow the spirit of the thing, I find this principle is the most useful for maintaining day-to-day discipline.

Keep memories electronically. Although the memories that our parents kept for us are very sweet, the volume of them is overwhelming. When I sorted through my memory boxes this fall, I found dozens of figure skating medals and reams of participation certificates. In thinking prospectively for our kids, we try to keep memories electronically. This means that we take pictures of items and ditch the originals instead of accumulating more fodder for the memory boxes. Goodbye ticket stubs, programs, menus, and, yes, the little ones' artwork. We have room for one work of art per child on the refrigerator, so pick your favorite, kiddo.

Maintain 30% extra space. Empty space begs to be filled. Yet, a home that is perfectly full, with no empty space, does not give room for growth. I vaguely remember reading a Feng Shui article that suggested you need to leave empty space in your home in order for good things to arrive. Our target is that any closet, cupboard, or drawer can be up to 70% filled and should remain at least 30% empty. This is admittedly a tough one, but it's always a good reminder for me when I am tempted to shove the nth t-shirt in the drawer.

Let it go. When an item can serve others better than it can serve you, pass it on swiftly and without hesitation.

This can be difficult for us because we're both so frugal. That said, as we sold our San Francisco apartment and moved across the country to a Connecticut rental, we were reminded how owning, maintaining, and moving items requires the expenditure of real mental and physical energy. Instead of hoarding "value" by keeping things that we are unlikely to use again, we try to do the more comprehensive math of each item's value to us, weighing our likelihood to use it versus the more intangible costs of ownership. This is not exactly Marie Kondo's approach of disposing of things if they don't bring you joy, but it has a similar ruthlessly cleansing result.

Since originally articulating our approach, we have also added new principles related to how we manage our stuff with kids.

Up to one toy. Both to manage our space and also to keep ourselves sane, we limit friends and family to giving "up to one toy" for holidays and birthdays. They are welcome to give an endless parade of books, clothes, and college fund contributions, but zero or one toy only. Sometimes little things sneak through (particularly if they're consumable, like crayons, stickers, or bath bombs), and we're okay with that. The point is that we are trying to set limits upon the endless consumption of things. Our goal is making our boundaries clear with others and providing some of that discipline to our children as well.

Want/Need/Wear/Read. I can't remember where we picked this one up, but before Elliott's first Christmas, we decided that she would receive four and only four gifts from us for the holiday: something she wants, something she needs, something to wear, and something to read. The small number and clear categories keep us from splurging on many things and force us to consider closely what we acquire.

As we step into the holiday season abundant with things—old things we're using and new things we're acquiring—this is a good moment to reflect on the intentionality of managing our possessions.

How do you manage your stuff?

What principles do you have for acquiring new things or dealing with what you have?

How can you bring more intention to this part of your life?

ALIGNING ACTIONS
WHILE PLANNING

Regardless of what you are doing, the most pragmatic way of aligning your actions to your ambitions is by simply planning to do so. Harnessing your to-do list to become more intentional is a core trick here. Ultimately, your to-do list can support you in not only doing what you want to do, but also being who you want to be.

APRIL 17, 2016
SAN FRANCISCO, CALIFORNIA

I've often considered this question: How do I embed intentional action into everyday life?

In 2013, I experimented with creating an accountability checklist. It included space for everything from hours slept to minutes meditated. It included a reminder to send notes to everyone who had a birthday that day, a place to mark down how many outstanding messages were in my Gmail and Outlook, and a check box to indicate whether I flossed. Not every ambition was achievable each day, and equally important, not every one of them was resonant every day. As the months passed, I realized that although my list included many worthy goals, I was layering on accountability for more and more to-dos, rather than accounting for how I wanted to be.

Suddenly, the question was more complex. It was not only a question of how I would embed intentional action into my everyday, but also a question of how I would embed intentional action when it reflected the nebulous "ways I wanted to be" instead of the more tangible "things I wanted to do?"

My solution, and one that has naturally stuck for a couple of years now, was to make a "to be" list when I make my daily "to do" list. If you're anything like me, writing a to-do list comes naturally; my brain cannot account for everything that needs to get done, so I write it all down. This became a natural departure point for the ways I wanted to be. Here is my approach (repeated daily).

First, I list all my *calendar items for the day*. These are my fixed commitments. From meetings to appointments to social events, they're unlikely to move. This provides me with an idea of how much additional time remains.

Second, I list all my *to dos*. What are the other things I need to accomplish today? Sometimes this is a long list of mini-tasks, sometimes it is bigger blocks of thinking work that need space. My calendar helps determine what's possible. For example, if I lack a stretch longer than thirty minutes, I won't be able to make progress against my bigger tasks in that amount of time. Thus, I will either break down big tasks into reasonable pieces, or I won't put them on today's list at all. This helps me narrow my focus to what's realistically doable today.

So far, this sounds like a fairly normal approach.

The difference comes in the last step. Finally, I add my *to be* list to the same piece of paper. This connects my overarching personal development goals to the realities of today. I consider where am I headed, who I'm becoming, and what skills I'm trying to build to get me there. With this big ambition in mind, I look at my emerging list. The intersection of my long-term aspirations and everyday realities gives me a handful of ideas of how I want to show up on that day in particular. For example:

If I have a lot of calls, I might add, "Listen intently and be fully present,"

If I see a block of time in the evening with less to do, I might add, "Make time to connect with Liz tonight."

If I have lots of thinking work to do and am afraid that I'll become too caught up in my head, I might add, "Be connected to my body."

If I see a one-on-one meeting with someone on my team, I might add, "Show compassion and love."

Happily, the bullet points I put on my to-be list rarely add more things to do. Instead, they inform *how* I act while going about my day.

The power of the to-be list comes from setting micro-intentions about how to be and embedding them in the reality of your day-to-day.

How do you track your goals
on a day-to-day basis?

Who do you need "to be" in order to
accomplish your goals?

Thinking of tomorrow in particular,
what do you need to do and who do you need to be
to accomplish your goals?

WEDNESDAY

WORK
- ☐ Review team materials for Tuesday
- ☐ Check on feedback survey
- ☐ Outline plan for September training
- ☐ Send follow-up emails to Asia offices
- ☐ Draft newsletter content

LIFE
- ☐ Update baby registry
- ☐ Schedule catch-up call with KC

TO DO

- Be fully present (one-on-one calls, lunch with kids)
- Stay connected to my body and move through my day (pool, yoga)
- When in doubt, be more loving

TO BE

- Walk dog
- Morning yoga
- 7AM Global check-in
- 8AM Call with Sarah
- 8:30AM Call with Melissa

- 11AM team check-in

- 12:00PM Liz lunch

CALENDAR

- 4:00 PM Doctor's appointment

- Pick up kids

© whipple callahan, 2019

Your Evolved To-Do List

CHOOSING MINDSETS

We all operate within a world delimited by our beliefs. We tell ourselves, "That won't work," "I'm too good for this job," or "It's unacceptable to act that way." Our world changes when we realize that these beliefs—and the mindsets they are built on—are not absolutely true. Yes, what we believe is relative.

Our mindsets are the result of our experiences in the world, shaped by our social conditioning and compounded by our cognitive biases. These biases—and confirmation bias in particular—cause us to reconfirm our mindsets instead of seeking new data. Over time, these mindsets become invisible to us. They become the lens through which we see the world, and, much like a pair of glasses, it's easy to forget that we're wearing them.

Living within the mindsets accidentally formed through our haphazard experience is simply another form of living incidentally. Just as we intentionally choose our actions, so may we intentionally choose our mindsets. This takes first seeing the mindsets we have—essentially, taking off the glasses that we wear and examining the lenses. Then, we must consciously test those mindsets versus reality and choose mindsets that are both true and useful to our goals. Since action springs from thought, and thought is limited by mindsets, aligning actions to ambitions requires adjusting mindsets as well. Thereby, reworking our mindsets is one of the most powerful actions we can take in acting intentionally.

CHOOSING MINDSETS
ABOUT JUDGMENT

You may be surprised to learn just how much latitude you have to characterize the world around you. When you see that nothing is inherently good or bad, you simultaneously gain the ability to choose your orientation for yourself.

JULY 29, 2014

SAN FRANCISCO, CALIFORNIA

"I wonder if you know what it means to be aware of something? Most of us are not aware because we have become so accustomed to condemning, judging, evaluating, identifying, choosing. Choice obviously prevents awareness because choice is always made as a result of conflict. To be aware ... just to see it, to be aware of it all without any sense of judgment."
    -Jiddu Krishnamurti

I've been inclined to judge lately. I don't mean I've been judgmental from a moral perspective, such as gossiping about people, failing to be compassionate, or struggling with empathy. Instead, I've been doing a lot of the innocent form of judging we do every day.

I've been looking at things and saying, This is good, and that is bad. I like this, and I don't like that. I will take this one, and I don't want that one. At a higher level, my assessments start to look more like plans and ambitions with judgments hidden inside them: I want more of this, I want less of that. We are on-track, we are off-track.

Making these assessments seems to be an easy (and fairly non-controversial) matter.

Aren't they obvious? (*Of course,* breaking your leg is bad.)

Aren't they generally agreed upon? (*Everyone* hates getting stuck in traffic.)

Furthermore, aren't they useful? (I don't like getting burned, so I will stay in the shade.)

From a pragmatic perspective, judgment is necessary. We wouldn't function in the world unless we were willing to make assessments and take action. From a broader perspective, though, there are three issues with judgment that I sometimes forget:

First, as Krishnamurti points out above, sometimes we lack awareness because we are so quick to judge. We don't take the moment of presence without judgment before we determine if a rose is beautiful or ugly. When we decide how we feel about it so quickly, we miss the opportunity to just be aware of a situation.

Second, when we judge without that window of awareness, we forget that we are judging at all. We go quickly from seeing the world to asserting our judgments of it. It's not that we saw a rose and judged it ugly; we simply saw an ugly rose. We lose consciousness that judgment happens.

Third, when we move straight to judgment, those judgments often become capital-T Truths to us. In reality, all of our assessments are flexible. None are necessarily right; almost all are, in some cases, wrong. They look correct from some angles and wrong from other angles. The rose that is ugly in a bouquet of lively blooms could be poignantly beautiful in a memento mori setting, when the message is, "Remember you must die." Time, place, and situation play a role in determining the "correctness" of our assessment. An old Taoist fable illustrates this point.

> *There was an old farmer who lived on a farm with his family, his crops, and his horse. One day, his horse ran away. Upon hearing the news, his neighbors came to visit.*
>
> *"Ahh, what bad luck!" they said sympathetically.*
>
> *"Maybe," the farmer replied.*

The next day, the horse returned, bringing with it three other wild horses. Again, the neighbors came to visit.

"Ahh, what good luck!" they exclaimed.

"Maybe," the farmer replied.

The day after, the farmer's son tried to ride one of the untamed horses. He was thrown from the horse and broke his leg. Again, the neighbors came to visit.

"Ah, what bad luck!" they said sympathetically.

"Maybe," the farmer replied.

The following day, military officials came to the village to draft young men into the army. Because the son's leg was broken, they passed by him. The neighbors again came to visit.

"Ahh, what good luck!" they exclaimed.

"Maybe," the farmer replied.

Bringing it back to my little, less rural world, I ask myself, *Is my line up of conference calls today good or bad? Is it positive or negative that my friend cancelled dinner tomorrow? Is it good or bad that the dog puked on the carpet last night?*

I'm trying to remind myself that there's no judgment inherent in any of it. It all just is, and the judgment I apply to it is entirely my own creation.

How do you judge what is good and bad in your life?

How do you know that your judgments are true?

What if what you thought was bad is actually good?
And vice versa?

CHOOSING MINDSETS
ABOUT THE NEW

When you look around you, what do you see? When faced with a new situation, do you judge it through the lens of your previous experiences? Or, do you stay open and curious, endeavoring to understand these new inputs more independently? You can choose this mindset. With consciousness, you can set aside your own history and approach new experiences on their own merits.

NOVEMBER 8, 2014
NEW DELHI, INDIA

This past week, I spent at least two hours a day driving across Rajasthan, Haryana, and Delhi states. Although driving is a universal task, driving in India differs from what I expect in three major ways.

First and most evident, the traffic conventions are unique. Drivers practice speedy passing and have minimal regard to lanes. It's not unusual to dodge an oncoming truck, even on a divided highway, when you might assume that the truck should be on the opposite side of the barrier. Plenty of slow-moving objects (e.g., donkeys, tractors, horses, cows, bicycles) share the highway, and horns punctuate the majority of driving maneuvers.

Second, because of these conventions, driving in India takes distinct skill. I've always had a driver when I've come to the country (daring to drive only once in Calcutta—and then for maybe a block). This means that I'm almost always in the passive passenger role instead of the active driver role.

Third, there just seems to be a lot of driving. Over the past week, I've spent over a day of it (yes, twenty-four hours) in the car. Four and one-half hours here. Three hours there. Thirty minutes that was supposed to be five minutes, but we got caught behind a gaggle of schoolkids drumming and then had a run-in with a camel.

Collectively, this makes driving in India quite different from the States. You spend a lot of time in a car, over which you have minimal control, and you may feel explicitly out of control when your driver makes the nth harrowing dodge-and-weave move around a formidable truck.

In reaction to these differences, I've heard every possible reaction. Some visitors complain, "Ugh, the traffic is awful! It took us six hours to get to Agra!" Others say, "I loved all our visits, but my favorite part was in the car, just watching the world go by."

I'm no exception. My own experience of driving just this week ranged from:

- "Hurrah for driving! What a wonderful way for me to reintegrate back into India. I'll watch the world go by, read the *Times of India*, and get my head back into being here."
- "Driving is the worst. I don't want to make small talk with anyone and think my head is going to explode." Note: We stopped halfway through this drive for me to throw up. Good times.
- "This can be fun as well as educational. I'll sit next to my new friend and work on learning the Hindi alphabet so I can read the signs."
- "Driving is the worst. I'm so done with this. I will personally get out and push the cow off the road if that's what needs to happen here."
- "How lovely to have this time to discuss—to debrief, to digest, to talk about things that really matter."
- "Why are we stopped? . . . No, seriously, why are we stopped?"

When I hate driving, I really hate driving. I am viscerally tied up in my frustration and annoyance. And when I love driving, I really love driving. I am compelled by the country, happy to chat with a friend, and completely at ease about how long everything takes. The bad is objectively bad, and the good is objectively good.

Yet, in reality, driving in India is neither good nor bad. It just is. My experience is simply what I decide to bring to the situation. My reaction to the blaring horns and gridlocked cars is just the result of the experiences I've had, the opinions I've formed, and the reality I decide to buy into at any given time.

The same is true with every experience in life: traffic, changes of plans, a promotion, a death, the breakfast menu, that music blaring, the room I'm assigned at the hotel, an illness. We often buy into broad assumptions of good or bad (e.g., getting upgraded at the hotel yesterday is good, getting a migraine the other day is bad). Ultimately, though, none of these assessments are objectively true. For example, my upgraded room creeped me out because it was so big and old, and I slept with the lights on. The migraine, on the other hand, made me conscious about how I was engaging with other people and ensured I was fully present when I recovered.

Nothing is good or bad. It just is.

So thank you, India, for reminding me of this truth and giving me the choice of what to bring to the situation. As I prepare for yet more driving tomorrow, I am going to let myself believe that all that car time can be a blessing.

When did you assess a new experience based on your old, incomplete understanding the world?

What might you have missed in doing so?

When do you tend to judge situations?
When do you tend to stay open-minded?

CHOOSING MINDSETS
ABOUT LANGUAGE

Language is powerful. In Genesis, when given the ability to name the cattle, the birds of the sky, and the beasts of the field, Adam was, at the same moment, given dominion over them. Naming holds power. Given this power, we should carefully select the words we use to describe both ourselves and the things around us. Choosing our words intentionally subtly shapes how we experience the world.

MAY 31, 2015
SAN FRANCISCO, CALIFORNIA

The last weeks and months have been particularly *busy*. In the last six weeks, I've traveled to Shanghai, Chicago, Phuket, Boulder, Singapore, a tropical island in Indonesia, Cape Cod, and Michigan. I've camped the NorCal woods with my fiancée, snorkeled Southeast Asian waters, and taken a beer tour of Chicago. I've attended offsites, retreats, annual meetings, and trainings. I've coached former classmates on storytelling, tried a new recipe for macaroni and cheese, and volunteered at the soup kitchen. On the home front, we've replaced our washer and dryer, fixed the ice tray in the fridge (shockingly complicated), and replanted the front bed. For the wedding, we've ordered and addressed wedding invitations, finalized plans for cake, and completed the final fitting for my wedding dress. Most important, though, I've spent time with so many people I love around the world, including a few walks around the block with Reese, some quality time with Liz, and a beautiful bridal shower with nearly every member of my extended family.

I share this not to provide an excuse for not writing, but to take a stand: Yes, the last six weeks have been busy, but I refuse to call them that. In fact, *I am hereby abandoning the word "busy."*

Why am I abandoning "busy?"

First, *I don't want to compete in the busy-ness competition.* Sometimes, particularly among my overachieving friends, we end up one-upping each other with the intensity of our schedules. It's as if our commitments act as a proxy for importance ("So many people have demands on my time and talents!") and capability ("... and I'm completely able to satisfy them all!"). It's an alluring game to play because it feeds the ego and seems winnable. That said, winning the busy-ness competition is no treat. You may receive a bit of awe or pity, but to maintain your sense of importance and capability, you need to sign up for being even busier than you were before. I once heard a friend describe it as "winning a pie-eating competition where the prize is more pie."

Second, *I want to encourage real conversations.* We often ask each other "How are you doing?" in a ritualized way, not expecting a full answer. It's easy to reply, "I'm busy," and then share your schedule. When someone asks me how I'm doing, I aspire to respond to those questions with a better answer—one that goes deeper or shares more. Why am I busy? What is happening in the world as a result of my efforts? What can I share that might truly connect us?

Which brings us to the third and most important reason why I'm abandoning busy: *I want to put attention on the underlying meaning, not the superficial hum of the activity.* Ultimately, the word "busy" doesn't encapsulate the meaning behind it. We all choose to sign ourselves up for work and activities, for life and relationships. We choose the things that make us so busy, and we presumably choose them because they're important to us in some way. Being "busy" doesn't invoke the overarching purpose in the activity. It just implies activity—and perhaps too much of it. Yet, when I look at the litany of life in my first paragraph, I don't feel exhausted, I feel exhilarated. Sure, I'm sometimes over-traveled, sometimes overworked, sometimes overstretched. But my underlying feeling here is one of satisfying fullness, and not of meaningless busy-ness.

Therefore, that's my new word: instead of saying, "I'm busy," I am going to say "I'm full." I am full of activity, full of life, and full of meaning. In many contexts, to be full is to be complete. I want the fullness that comes with having my time and talents used completely toward my ambitions.

Goodbye to busy-ness. Welcome to fullness.

Do you feel busy or full?

Which of the things that make you busy give you meaning? Which of the things that make you busy lack meaning for you?

What do you want to do about it?

CHOOSING MINDSETS
ABOUT MOTIVES

When you see yourself as an actor in a situation, you are able to choose what role you will play. You can step back and examine your motivations. Are you acting for yourself? Are you acting for others? Like reflection on any lived experience, this reflection will both tell you something about yourself and also make available a new frontier of choice for how you act going forward. Ultimately, like an actor on the stage, you can choose the role you play and the motivations you bring to that role.

MARCH 5, 2017
SAN FRANCISCO, CALIFORNIA

As a parent, I want to optimize every situation for my baby's development. In addition to the feeding, diapering, snuggling, and bathing, I'm always at the ready with an age-appropriate toy or the Baby Einstein Pandora station. I read Wonder Weeks, Google every incremental action, and know the developmental milestones like the back of her tiny baby hand. But the other day, I was reminded of why I try to give Elliott space instead of trying to drive her development. This day in particular, I waited for her to turn from back to front. She had mastered the front-to-back roll but not the opposite.

Instead of entertaining her, showing her how to move, or even cheering her on, I got quiet. I watched the micro-movements that were not in her repertoire a couple of days earlier. She moved in a circle on her back to get a toy. She pushed off with her feet to scoot along on her back. She explored a blanket by putting it on her face instead of lying atop it. Eventually, after a long while, Elliott turned a full circle, 360 degrees, on her back. Looking at the babe, I realized that this wouldn't have happened if I had followed my instinct to reposition her as soon as she moved off her baby blanket or even changed her diaper as soon as I noticed it was wet. Instead, I let go of my parental agenda and followed her lead. She was exploring. She was happy. She had a wet diaper and was lying directly on the rug, but she was doing all sorts of unexpected and "untaught" things.

While I focused on the great big milestone of The Roll, Elliott was accomplishing a whole host of subtle new moves—when I gave her space to do so. Previously, by asking her to be with me instead of my being with her, I was missing all the ways she was developing herself, and I might have even been getting in her way.

In parenting, I have been particularly inspired by the thinking of Magda Gerber and her parenting philosophy known as *Resources for Infant Educarers* (or RIE). One key point of the philosophy is to "observe more, do less" and, correspondingly, to "do less, enjoy more."

I can go days feeding, changing, and playing with Elliott to belatedly realize that I've spent very little time just observing her. When I do that, I realize that she is up to far more interesting, complex, and developmentally appropriate "play" than I could ever design for her. It's not easy to settle and be present; Lee Fernandez, a RIE instructor we've worked with, suggested that even just ten minutes a day of truly being present to your baby is an accomplishment.

Of course, the following day, when Liz and I sat quietly with her, Elliott rolled from her back to her front. When she finally rolled over, she did it for a purpose. She turned over, not because I was showing her how to do it or cheering her on enthusiastically, but because she was exploring her world. She did it, not to satisfy some developmental milestone, but instead because it was the best way to reach her ball. Elliott had no sense of it being better to move this way or that way. Indeed, she seemed to be less likely to do what we might hope when we were getting in the way with our interference and expectations.

Now, when I'm shaking a toy in front of her face or moving a toy to within her reach, I have to ask myself, "Am I doing this for her or for me?" Often, I am trying to control the situation for me or shaking the toy to entertain myself. Instead, I need to breathe, take a step back, and see what she's doing. Ironically, that's the way that she ends up taking the developmental leaps that I am expecting anyway.

Which of your actions ostensibly done for others are really more for you?

Where in your life are you trying to force something to happen?

What would happen if you let it all unfold naturally?

CREATING MEANING

Crafting actions that are invested with deep intention is the third way to create alignment. In practice, this looks a lot like ritual. I am not referring exclusively—or even primarily—to the traditional ceremonies passed down in cultures or religions, but instead to the use of ritualized action. For example, when my family says what we're grateful for every night at dinner, we intentionally bring the value of gratitude to life through our words and actions. This is a more proactive and effortful approach as it often involves taking new actions with particular intent instead of simply aligning your existing actions to an ambition. Though—or perhaps because—it requires more effort, consciously creating meaning is a much more powerful approach for achieving alignment than the two previous alternatives.

CREATING MEANING THROUGH RITUAL

Rituals are everyday actions performed in a particular way in order to produce a certain result and invoke a certain meaning. They are a fantastic example of aligned action because all rituals are consciously intentional. Harnessing ritual action proactively embeds meaning in life.

NOVEMBER 25, 2015
SAN FRANCISCO, CALIFORNIA

When I was growing up, we always said grace before eating. Faster or slower, with more focus or more appetite, we said the following:

> "Lord, bless this food to our use and us to
> thy service,
> And make us ever-mindful of the needs of
> others. Amen."

Liz and I preserve the idea of grace, but we make it our own. Each night, when we sit down to dinner, we share gratitudes. It's a catalog of things we're grateful for on that day—everything from the meal, to getting a good night's rest, to the view out the window. In addition to the rotating set of things we appreciate, Liz always ends with "And I'm grateful for the puppy," at which point we look over to see Reese patiently sitting on the rug, mindful that he can't enter the dining room while we're eating. We then tuck into the meal and start up some everyday conversation about life.

These nightly gratitudes are daily, private, and modest. On the other hand, the upcoming holiday of Thanksgiving is annual, in community, and over the top. Thanksgiving asks us to not only reflect on gratitude, but to celebrate it. We cook it, share it with others, Instagram it, and gorge ourselves on it. Both rituals are lovely ways to embody gratitude.

When we sit down for an overabundance of food this year, our annual ritual of Thanksgiving and daily ritual of gratitudes will merge. While pouring far too much gravy over my entire plate, I'll share everything that I'm grateful for.

What are you grateful for?

What are your rituals (daily, weekly, annually)?
What meaning do they impart in your life?

What new rituals might you establish
to reflect your values?

CREATING MEANING
THROUGH SANCTIFICATION

Rituals need not be big to be powerful. Indeed, everyday actions provide opportunities to use differentiation and distinction to invest special meaning in simple things. The closest word we have to this, sanctification, is used typically in explicitly religious contexts. Call it sanctification, consecration, differentiation, specialization, or something else; it is simply the act of making something quite mundane actually very special by investing it with conscious, intentional meaning.

NOVEMBER 18, 2018
SAN JOSE, COSTA RICA

I was sitting around, chatting with a group of moms the other day. One friend mentioned that her son was not eating meals, and they were, as a result, putting in extraordinary effort to get him to do so. Her pediatrician's advice? Just "un-thing" it.

Un-thinging is the process of not making a big deal out of something. In other words, not making it into a thing. Her son can eat or not eat. Either is fine. As a parent, you set the direction and the implications (i.e., here is good food, you need to eat, or you'll be hungry), but you don't get tied up in what the child chooses to do. You don't bribe or coerce. You don't have an emotional reaction. You stay chill and let them figure it out independently. By un-thinging it, you lower the stakes. You normalize the situation. You create the space and opportunity for choice and change.

In becoming conscious of un-thinging things, we have also started to play around with thinging things. By thinging something, you differentiate it. You make clear that the behavior is situational and even special. You create limits and boundaries around it. For example, when flying with my toddler the other day, we decided to thing the use of a diaper. My daughter is in the middle of potty training, and we don't want her to think that wearing a diaper is typical behavior. So, my wife drew airplanes on each of her diapers. We talked about how these were special "plane diapers." When we took off the diapers, we said goodbye to the them and made a big deal of wearing underwear again because we were not on a plane anymore. We made diaper-wearing during travel a thing.

Beyond that, we are thinging a whole host of behaviors associated with travel, including lollipops to pop her ears on the plane ("plane lollipops"), the use of a tablet ("special Daniel Tiger"), eating more frequent desserts ("something we do on vacation"), and sleeping on an inflatable mattress ("your older toddler bed"). We want each to be a specific experience with its own use case, boundaries, and related expectations. We are creating the association that these are all related to this special time and place and do not reflect the new normal.

Stepping back, thinging and unthinging are simply more intentional practices about consciously choosing—and in this case, consciously choosing your relationship with each action.

What have you made into a thing in your life?

What do you need to unthing to create space
and opportunity for change?

What else could you thing to create differentiation
and limitation?

CREATING MEANING
THROUGH TRADITION

Traditions are repeated actions that compound meaning based on both the intent behind the tradition and also the frequency with which it is repeated. Without requiring much conscious effort, well-designed traditions can help us live intentionally each time they recur, inviting us deeper and deeper into meaning.

DECEMBER 25, 2014
RICHFIELD, MINNESOTA

Given that we're recently engaged, this is the first holiday season Liz and I have fully merged our travel plans. We spent Thanksgiving with my family in Michigan and Christmas with hers in Iowa and Minnesota. While navigating each other's traditions, we're also intentionally creating our own. Although we celebrated Christmas today with Liz's mother, sister, and brother-in-law, we celebrated our own Christmas last Friday and Saturday before leaving San Francisco. Friday was our faux Christmas Eve, and Saturday was our stand-in Christmas Day. We knew we would participate in our respective family traditions when we traveled, so this would be the place where we started our own traditions—some adopted from her family, some adopted from mine, some merged, some imagined anew.

Our Friday night "Christmas Eve" consisted of a celebratory dinner, cozy fire, and loitering on the couch, listening to Christmas music. We experimented with prime rib, twice-baked potatoes, corn, and a kale salad for dinner, trying to figure out whether that felt like our holiday meal. Following Liz's family tradition, we each opened one present (a puzzle for her, hot chocolate for me). And following my family tradition, we sprinkled "fairy dust" in the fireplace to help Santa ease down the chimney.

Christmas morning, we awoke lazily and settled onto the couch with our respective caffeine of choice (Diet Coke for Liz and coffee for me). We opened presents methodically, one-for-her and one-for-me until the pile had disappeared. I was surprised to find that even small acts like this are loaded with invisible decisions (e.g., Do we wrap presents for each other? Does Santa wrap his presents? Do we open all at once or do we go back and forth?). It's been curious to not only experience different ways of doing things as I step into Liz's family, but to also figure out which of the traditions I care about. I mind less whether we have a real or artificial tree, but I care immensely that we use the stockings that my grandmother knitted (including new ones for Liz and Reese).

Christmas morning breakfast was perhaps our easiest tradition to establish. On special days in the past (i.e., holidays, the morning of our engagement), we ate a crescent-roll-scrambled-egg creation we dubbed Miracle Loaf. As with many rituals, we can't quite remember why we eat it or why it has that name, but at this point, it's stuck. This year, we evolved the Miracle Loaf recipe further, adding garlic, replacing green onions with white onions, and slap-dashing some egg wash on top to brown it up. It is perhaps the first true Whipple/Callahan creation in our recipe collection.

Like me, you may be asking "What does it all mean?" "What values do our traditions manifest?" and "What do our traditions aspire to?" For the most part, I don't think we've created these traditions because they are specifically meaningful or symbolic. Instead, we select some to honor her heritage, we select some to honor my heritage, and then we co-create together. The meaning is less in the action of eating the Miracle Loaf or wrapping the gifts, but instead in the fact that we're consciously creating our own traditions together.

What traditions does your heritage give you?

Which do you embrace, and which do you discard or reinvent?

How do you craft new, intentional traditions?

This brings us to the end of Chapter Three, *Alignment*. While the concept of aligning what you want with what you do may seem simple, the dimensions of actions, mindsets, and meaning are dizzyingly complex. And so, as we close the chapter, I want to sort through it in a more straightforward way. Before moving on, stop here and reflect on three simple closing questions:

What ideas resonated most with you?

Where do you see the greatest opportunity to align what you do with what you want in your life?

What is one change you might make to live in greater alignment?

CHAPTER FOUR

SURRENDER

Living in this way—with such intention—may seem constraining and exhausting. Isn't it a significant cognitive load to think constantly about how you're acting? And isn't it hard to live within a tight vision of who you are and what you want?

It's a mistake to think that, simply because you are intentional, you are micro-managing your life. Intentionality is not a matter of being in control or perpetuating the illusion that you had control in the first place. We are not and have never been in control of our lives.

Instead, intentionality is a matter of doing what you can do to live in a space of consciousness, reflection, and alignment and then releasing the rest. Become aware of living intentionally. Reflect upon what you do and why you do it. Attempt to align what you want and what you do. And then, *let go*.

Surrender is the unexpected but essential counterbalance to the controlling tendencies of intentionality. There is a duality in intentionality—this interplay between control and surrender. To live intentionally, you need to exert your influence over what you can control and to do so thoughtfully. At the same time, you must abandon expectations, let go of plans, and, in many ways, give up your very self. It is only by letting go that your intentional life will come into focus.

SURRENDER YOUR CONTROL

The most frequent mistake I make is thinking that I'm in control in this life. It trips me up time and time again. But, slowly, over time, I am learning how important it is for me to hold tightly to my ambitions while letting go of how they will be fulfilled.

AUGUST 4, 2014
SAN FRANCISCO, CALIFORNIA

Sometimes I get stuck in a feeling of lack. It could be lacking anything—enough money, enough time, the right attitude, the right opportunities, the perfect interactions with others. Like everyone, I find myself assessing that, "This is not enough," and, "That is not right."

This weekend, I was throwing away junk mail when I ran across a flier from a self-help program. In my cursory flip through, I found this suggestion.

"Get in touch with the feeling of what's it's like to feel you have your every need and want already met."

Every need and want already met. That sounds nice, I thought. *Impractical, but nice.*

It continued in the same manner.

"Just rest into that feeling for a moment. Feel it in your belly. Allow it to expand up into your heart. Open up your awareness to feeling it spread all throughout every cell in your body and even to the area around your body."

Of course, it sounds cheesy. It is *absolutely* cheesy. But I try not to let judgments like that limit my experience, so I gave it a shot.

I opened up my journal and wrote down everything I needed and wanted: a perfectly-balanced travel schedule, the willpower to follow through on my health commitments, a thriving social life that is both broad and deep, and a perfect and cheaper-than-expected wedding venue.

This exercise of envisioning the future was not unfamiliar to me; my journals are filled with goals, expectations, and ambitions. What felt different about this, however, was experiencing those ambitions from the perspective of "already-havingness" and "already-beingness" instead of plotting how they would occur in the future.

You see, when I set a goal, my instinct is to write a tactical plan that outlines exactly how I'll get there. So, when I set the vision of a "perfect and cheaper-than-expected wedding venue," I was quick to start my Excel spreadsheet of locations, ask former brides for their suggestions, and fire up the online diligence. When faced with a goal, I default to strategic thinking, clever problem solving, and execution prowess to get me there. These are my trusty old tools; I'm good at them, and, most of the time, they work.

This challenge to experiment with already-havingness and already-beingness eviscerated my typical approach. I had to turn off the achievement machine in my head. No more mental to-do lists, no more clever plans to bring my goals to life. Instead, I just had to sit, to let them come, to feel them to be true with every part of my body. And it felt amazing.

Beyond feeling good (many things make you feel good, and this is just one), it seemed to be useful as well. Case-in-point. As soon as I gave up the spreadsheet, the appointments, and the aggressive pre-planning, we locked down our perfect, cheaper-than-expected wedding venue. The already-havingness was, weirdly, already true.

Do I believe that you can imagine your goals into existence? Not necessarily. Still, it's both wonderful and relieving to think that every good thing doesn't need to be the result of my effortful striving. A better approach for me might be to let go just a bit. Stop trying to drive so much. Stop trying to work so hard. And maybe join together my vigorous action to make things happen with the faith and feeling that they already have.

Do you typically default to making it happen or letting it come?

What are the benefits of your approach?
What are the drawbacks?

Where can you benefit from stepping into the other perspective?

SURRENDER YOUR EFFORTS

Intentionality comes to life, as quoted in the essay below, "where trying and not trying meet." I wish you not only intentionality, but also its important counterparts: effortlessness, spontaneity, flow, joy, and ease.

OCTOBER 10, 2014
SAN FRANCISCO, CALIFORNIA

I've realized that I'm always trying. Trying to do, trying to be. Trying, trying, trying.

The whole idea of trying has value to me because I believe that I have agency—a lot of agency. When I work toward my goals with enthusiasm, intelligence, and emotional awareness, my efforts are typically correlated with results. All my experience supports this. I send emails, stuff happens. I make slides, stuff happens. I talk to someone on the phone, stuff happens. It's a pretty straightforward view of the world. Further, it's a view of the world that has allowed me to be happy and successful to date. Keep trying, and there will be success.

But what happens when I don't try?

When a friend asked me that question last weekend, it unleashed an avalanche of defensiveness and self-justification. "Not trying?! That's inconceivable!" huffed The Defensive One in my head. (I imagine him wearing an old-school British barrister outfit as he argues each point.) "That's an incredible betrayal! It controverts the very idea of intentionality, one of your core values!" He gets only more flustered and riled as he continues. "For heaven's sake, why invite the Queen to tea if you're not going to show up?"

It's true. After observing the effort/result correlation enough times, I've been duped into believing that voice. I've come to see that the world moves forward when I try—and therefore, I have convinced myself I must keep trying.

So what happens when I don't try? With this worldview, presumably nothing. And yet, I increasingly observe that's not, in fact, the case.

This Wednesday was a good example. I worked all day developing a new piece of training content, figuring out the flow of the module and tailoring each exercise so it would serve the learning goal. I sat in front of my computer, revising text, swapping slides, changing pictures. As I finished the day, I had the sense that something was mildly off. I decided to step back, take a break, and go for a pedicure.

Thus, I found myself an hour later, sitting in the pedicure chair, feet in a shallow pool of water and journal on my lap. I was writing about whatever craziness I typically journal on. And I was giving myself a self-congratulatory pat-on-the-back for creating time for self-care. But then, with three of ten toes bright orange, I realized, *Ahh! I know exactly what needs to change in that module! I see how to reformulate the question to really make it sing.*

I've worked for so long under the belief that my efforts, directly exerted upon the task at hand, will create the most movement. Still, I'm learning that sometimes there's more movement when you stop trying and let things be effortless. This isn't just true because the subconscious parts of my brain get a chance to process the information (as in this example), but also because things external to me seem to work in a different way when I stop trying as well. People line up to support a new idea. Someone sends an email with the information I need. A new offer comes to the table. It sounds crazy and semi-magical, but something happens when I stop trying. And much of the time, that force moves the world forward more powerfully than my efforts ever could.

So here's my challenge. I am going to try to stop trying. Or, phrased more positively, I am going to see if I can relax and let go. That way, I may just find my way to that productive and elusive place where trying and not trying meet.

What are your beliefs around"trying hard"
and "letting go?"

What happens when you let go?

Where in your life do you need to let go right now?

SURRENDER YOUR PLANS

Even the best laid plans are often thwarted by reality. Intentionality need not be abandoned when you encounter resistance. Instead, take all perceived setbacks as opportunities to reflect more deeply. You will learn more about the world and yourself. And you will emerge better able to realign what you want and what you do.

SEPTEMBER 3, 2014
SEOUL, SOUTH KOREA

Like many people experimenting with health, I spent the last month eliminating sugar from my diet. I didn't expect much of a challenge. I've never had a sweet tooth, and I would always choose a bag of chips over a candy bar. That said, this month without sugar was plenty tough and highly insightful. My realizations after swearing off sugar:

First, *sugar is elusive—and pervasive.* I fielded a lot of hard-to-answer questions as I started this month. "Are you giving up sweets, fruit, or both?" "What about sugar as an additive?" "Do you count agave?" "What about corn syrup?" "Are you ready to spend a third of your life reading labels?" At the beginning, I'll admit that I didn't have a sophisticated plan of attack. I thought I'd simply omit sugar as I had dairy the month prior. As I started down that path, however, I realized how close to impossible that would be. Not only are white sugar, brown sugar, powdered sugar, demerara sugar, and the other straight-forward sugars in question. No. In just my first trip to the grocery store, I realized the many other names that sugar takes. Not only does sugar masquerade as high fructose corn syrup (made from corn instead of cane, but with similar effects), it goes by evaporated cane juice as well. "Organic evaporated cane juice?" you say. "Isn't that essentially organic...juice? It sounds so good for you!" But alas, whether they evaporate it, centrifuge it, or crystallize it, it is indeed sugar. And that culprit is in basically every organic processed food product lining the Whole Foods shelves. Although I set high ambitions, I ended up scaling them back to the easiest of all possible paths (avoiding sugar-focused items, but allowing added sugar and fruits) within only the first few days. Even though I took the least rigorous path, it would still get tougher.

Second, *sugar helps us share meaningful experiences with others.* Do you want a slice of my birthday cake? Will you commiserate with me over a bowl of ice cream? Will you have a cookie my aunt baked? If alcohol is a social lubricant that eases awkwardness, sugar is the ingredient that punctuates the highs and lows of life. Every time something is particularly celebratory, there's sugar (birthday cake! wedding cake! every other type of cake!). Every time something is particularly sad, there's sugar (the proverbial pint of ice cream at a break-up). We make and share sweets to show our love, affection, or friendship, as symbolized by the cupcakes offered me by a friend at work. We find solace in sweets when the day is done. Whatever the occasion, avoiding sugar felt tantamount to denying the most meaningful moments of life. This month alone I faced multiple wedding cakes, a birthday ice cream social, and ritualistic Labor Day s'mores around the campfire. For someone who is not only an extrovert, but also so focused on meaning, this was a crushing challenge. It wasn't the sugar itself, but instead what the sugar symbolized that challenged me. It's nearly impossible to celebrate with equal fervor (or have other people see you as sincerely participating) when they're all eating cake, and you're munching on kale.

So, my overall conclusion? Because of both the practical difficulty of avoiding its many incarnations and the social tax of giving it up, *avoiding sugar is exhausting* for me.

But let's be honest. Those weren't the big insights. I had figured out both of those realities by the end of week one. By week two, the inherent difficulty of giving up sugar and the social implications of limiting it were not the only things that made the wheels fall off this resolution. Aside from both of these, something else was going on as well.

What happened when those desserts kept coming? There were, of course, the voices in my head that said, "No, Meredith, you can't have that ice cream!" and, "Bad Meredith, why are you eating a doughnut?" And worse, "Meredith, you are disappointing not only yourself with this brownie, but everyone you told about this diet!" I felt exactly the way I had when I'd screwed things up in the past—by making grand pronouncements about what I was going to do and then changing my mind along the way. And because I wrote about my intention on my blog, the voices came up stronger and louder than I've ever heard a chorus of self-blaming, dessert-shunning voices sound.

I set forth the goal of trying a new limitation each month and reporting back on how it went. It was going to be a beautiful little lifestyle project. I thought that whatever I chose for the month, it would be reasonable to control just that one thing: not eating sugar, or dairy, or whatever. It's not that I lacked the willpower;

I've been doing P90X every day and eating better than I ever have. In fact, I lost seven pounds this last month. It's not that I lacked the mindfulness; I've been increasingly conscious of what I eat and when I eat it. But beyond the challenges I shared above, the reality is that life didn't fit into my perfectly symmetrical plan. Life happened, it happened differently from what I expected, and I couldn't control it.

While I was supposed to focus on eliminating sugar, I suddenly felt myself drawn to counting calories. I don't know why. I've never done it before. I just resonated with exercising discipline around food in a different way, and I went from focusing on limitation to playing with allocation.

Being open to shifting my approach was freeing in many ways. Limitation, which was the central idea behind my wedding diet, put me in a place of saying a categorical no to some foods, and to others, thinking, *Sure, but I'll probably give it up next month.* The result was a halo of no around most foods. This created a collectively negative way of seeing food. Playing an allocation game, on the other hand, was much more positive. I could eat all sorts of things, but there were bounds as to what moderation meant.

I hoped that I would achieve greater awareness of my body and a sustainable approach to eating by following my diet plan. So much of me wants to shoehorn my life back into that perfect project plan I made for it. When I take a broader view, however, I see that I'm achieving the outcome I wanted, just via a different path. If thinking about allocation instead of limitation works for me, why would I deny that insight? I feel great, and I've been able to do that while eating cake at weddings.

So, the month without sugar has also became the month without control. I can set ambitions, but I don't always have perfect control over how I get there. If I can live with that human messiness, maybe what I realized this month can also push me in the direction of greater self-love and growing connection to my body, which is what I was searching for all along.

When have you had to abandon a plan?

How did you feel?

What did you learn as a result?

SURRENDER YOUR EXPECTATIONS

It's easy to impose expectations upon yourself. These expectations may come from your family, your friends, your society, or even from you. Without realizing what you're doing, you internalize these voices and force yourself to live within their limitations. You will only come to thrive when you are able to put them down and create the space to live outside them.

FEBRUARY 9, 2016
SAN FRANCISCO, CALIFORNIA

Let's start with the headline: I'm pregnant. Fifteen weeks. Due July 25. Don't know the sex yet but will find out. Going to stay in our current house. Don't have a name yet. And yes, our dog, Reese, is very pleased.

That's the explanation for my blogging hiatus. It's been ten weeks and six days since I've blogged. That is ten weeks and six days of feeling crappy.

Since the positive pregnancy test, my entire lifestyle flipped on its head. I went from keeping a primarily dairy-free, gluten-free, organic, minimally processed diet to developing the appetite of a toddler. Most of my meals involved chicken tenders. I started eating hard candy. I could not get enough cheese and bread. Being a rational adult, I did try to sneak some cooked kale into my macaroni and cheese, but I couldn't dupe myself and picked it out. Similarly, my sleeping habits shifted. I typically get eight hours of sleep and then turn into a whirlwind of productivity during the day. Now, I found myself ready to clock up to ten hours a night and cherishing a mid-day nap. Moving my body in any way sounded miserable. Leaving the house was not on my list of things to do. My wife, Liz, wondered if it was the invasion of the body snatchers; I had been replaced by a lethargic look-alike.

My doctor, one of the few people who knew of my pregnancy, described it best: it's like having a constant low-grade hangover (except there's no fun night out and no miraculous revival when you finally get out of the woods).

All this caught me off guard. Sure, I have many close friends with babies, but I never fully realized how tough first trimester can be. Instead, my images of pregnancy were vibrant, lively, and (as it turns out) disproportionately second trimester. My Facebook feed abounded with pictures of smiling pregnant women who ran half-marathons, twisted into impressive yoga poses, and modeled for bump-centric photo shoots. They all had elated grins, silky hair, and more stylish clothes than I have ever worn. Even the pregnant ladies I met in person fit the mold: they ran seven miles a day, designed adorable bump-focused Halloween costumes, and munched on cucumbers when everyone else housed holiday sweets. In short, all the pregnant women I knew embodied the pregnancy glow.

I, on the other hand, was eating a mega-sized bag of gas station Doritos on my drive back from a doctor's appointment, pants unbuttoned. And this was only first trimester.

All this brought up two major emotions in me: self-blame and competition. First of all, why wasn't I doing a better job at being pregnant? What was wrong with me? Why was my body acting so strangely, and why was I giving into it? Second, I was resolved not to underperform at this pregnancy thing. What did they all have that I didn't have? What did I need to do to succeed at this?

In my life, I've become accustomed to the idea that thoughtful, diligent action drives results. Do the right work in high school and get into college. Do the right work in college and get a job. Do the right work in my job and craft the life I want.

But that's the thing I'm learning about pregnancy: *there is nothing to do.* My body's got it. Beyond taking some prenatals, cutting the booze, and moving a bit, I can't do much to influence the development of this baby. S/he is going to grow however s/he grows, whether I eat kale or cookies, whether I run a full marathon or watch a Netflix marathon. To be clear, I'm not giving up my responsibility. I'm just letting go of my control patterns a bit more.

Second trimester has provided more relief and normalcy. I eat vegetables again. I have fewer waves of nausea. I even started doing prenatal yoga like those ladies in the pictures. But I'm glad to have gone through the unexpected unpleasantness of first trimester. With this little one coming into the world, there will be only more and more things I can't control, from my child's feeding schedule, to the job s/he chooses after school. In that sense, this lesson in letting go is probably the healthiest thing I could do first trimester (aside from buying the organic version of chicken tenders).

When did you beat yourself up for not fulfilling an ideal to which you aspired?

What did you learn from that?

What is an ideal that you're trying to achieve now? Is that contributing to or detracting from your fulfillment?

SURRENDER YOUR HOPES

Reflection is the midwife of insight and learning. Yet, often the learnings gleaned from our experiences are completely different from what we hoped to learn. This was the case in giving birth to my second child, Hugh Archer.

OCTOBER 19, 2018
NORWALK, CONNECTICUT

One month ago, my son, Hugh Archer Whipple Callahan, came into the world.

Our little man was originally due on September 6, smack between our wedding anniversary and my birthday. Considering the advice that second children often come sooner than first and knowing my history of a late first arrival, Liz and I prepared ourselves to have a due date baby. Yes, he could be early or late, but the smart money (i.e., our midwife, our doula, our OB/GYN friends) put their bets on the "on-time" category, so we were ready. Not that there was much to prepare this time around. We knew how little he would need in the first few weeks, and we already had all the baby gear anyway.

His due date came and went. Day after day, we waited. Evenings brought increased fetal movement and thrills of excitement. Was tonight the night that I'd wake everyone up at 2 a.m. with labor pains? No. Morning after morning, I got up to report that I slept shockingly well; there was no baby. To encourage the little man along, I tried evening primrose oil, pineapple, bumpy car rides, pumping, eggplant Parmesan, acupressure, and red raspberry leaf tea, all to no avail.

Finally, at forty-one weeks and three days, I headed to the hospital for an induction. I felt strange arriving to the hospital in such a state of preparedness. Here we were, hospital bag in hand, no contractions yet, bellies full of breakfast, childcare in place, everyone calm. Based on Elliott's birth, I had come to see childbirth as a crazy ride of "expecting the unexpected." Curiously, the planful approach of an induction was so very expected that it felt even more unexpected to me.

I started on an IV drip of Pitocin and waited. At the time, I felt annoyed. After days of anticipation, the hours remaining grew even more difficult to bear. In retrospect, Sunday morning was a beautiful time to build relationships with the people who would attend my son's birth later that day. Looking back, I can see how, person by person, my crew slowly assembled. I started this whole adventure with Liz at my side. Aunt

Kate and Grandma both showed up in advance to take care of Elliott. They gave me the opportunity to yield last obligations and focus entirely on this birth. Then, upon arrival to the hospital, we added the labor and delivery nurse who started my IV and would finish the day coaching me through pushing. Soon my doula joined. She intuitively knew what I needed and was on my spiritual wavelength. Finally, the midwife, with decades of experience and lots of pragmatic love, arrived.

By the early afternoon, my contractions began, gently at first and then increasingly. Liz and I walked the halls haltingly, stopping every minute or so for a contraction. Each time a contraction came, I grasped my IV stand, picked a point on the wall for visual focus, and breathed through it. Thinking back on Elliott's birth, I remembered the contractions only as pain to be endured. This time, I felt them more as energy moving through me. It was almost as if spirit was pouring energy right into the top of my head, through my body, and out my vagina for the purpose of bringing this baby out with it. If I hesitated or resisted, that flowing energy would get stuck. If I let it simply course through me, it felt painful but also useful.

As I rode contraction after contraction and came to see that pain differently, I knew: This is what I had hoped for in childbirth. I had hoped to learn things about myself, about pain, about presence, about motherhood, and about life through labor. This was a fundamental human experience, consistent over the ages. I wanted to experience every aspect of it. I wanted to receive the wisdom of generations of women participating in this process. I wanted to see what I would learn from it and how I might evolve. My underlying assumption was that I would learn the most by having a natural birth; drugs would disrupt and obscure what I was meant to experience.

Yet as the birth progressed, my fears crept in. My biggest fear was not the pain of the current contraction; I had found my way to be present to that. Instead, my biggest fear was the expectation of where those contractions might go. How much longer would this take? How much more intense would it be? Would I be able to be stand the sensations? How much did I believe in myself? Aspirationally, I wanted to do all of it without drugs. I wanted to trust in nature and to believe in myself that much.

But I didn't. Eventually, my question turned from whether I would be able to withstand the pain to why I was choosing to experience it in the first place. While laboring on all fours on the bed, I uttered out loud, "Why am I doing this?" for all to hear. *Why am I bearing such pain when there are options for relief? Is it better for me? Better for the baby? Is there really some great spiritual insight to uncover?*

Around six or seven centimeters, I got an epidural. Part of me is still tempted to judge myself for doing so. I feel that if only had I been stronger, braver, more spiritually centered, then I would have had the capacity to be with the experience. Yet, I have to let that go. As in all life experiences, my learnings came, not from running some externalized gauntlet (in this case, giving birth naturally). Instead, learnings came from being present to the experience right in front of me and the struggle that it prompted inside of me. My real insights came from seeing how an expected plan can still feel unexpected, from challenging my views of necessary and unnecessary suffering, from reconciling the coexistence of spiritual fullness and modern medicine in my mind, and from examining my assumptions of where and how spiritual growth occurs. Ultimately, it was not about some womanly secret revealed only if I endured; it was about me in the here and now.

Labor progressed swiftly from that point, and by early evening, I was ready to push. At that point, a fair amount of assistance was required to ultimately deliver the little man into the world, but this was of less of concern to me. By that time, I wasn't focused on my learning anymore. I was focused on having a healthy baby, and it was time for the little man to come out.

And so, my son joined us at 7:05 that night, as healthy as could be. He had none of the complications that Elliott experienced (meconium in the amniotic fluid, jaundice shortly after birth). In the month since his birth, he's proven even stronger. He's made breastfeeding easy, he's gained weight at a remarkable rate, and he's even giving us some reasonable opportunities to sleep.

So welcome to the world, my little Hawk (a nickname derived from his initials, HAWC). In giving birth to you, I learned new lessons beyond those I learned giving birth to Elliott. The experiences may be similar, but the edges of learning are all new and unique. I know that I'll continue to learn new and different things from parenting you as you grow. I'm excited for this journey together with our whole family.

When have you held strong expectations of what you were supposed to learn from an experience?

How did that go?

What did you learn instead?

SURRENDER YOUR ASPIRATIONS

Intentionality can turn into a futile and frustrating process if you grasp too tightly to a particular vision of what you want. To live with not only intentionality, but also wisdom, you must be flexible. You must learn about what is currently possible and not possible in your world. And you must be willing and able to shift your ambitions in the face of this reality.

NOVEMBER 27, 2018

ARENAL, COSTA RICA

When we told friends and family we would be traveling through Costa Rica for the last two months of my maternity leave, we got a lot of interesting reactions. Some were in disbelief, thinking us either crazy or stupid for taking a two-month newborn and a two-year toddler anywhere. Others were jealous of the idea and seemed almost annoyed that they didn't organize something similar with their own children. Still others couldn't wrap their minds around the complexity of it all (logistical and otherwise) and surmised that we must be superhuman (fact: my wife is).

Now, two weeks into the trip, we get a lot of curious questions from people on the home front who want to know how it's going. The tone is often tentative, almost as if people are wishing us well but expecting a train wreck. "So…how is it?"

When I began to answer that question, I measured my answer against two things: our ideal of traveling and our ideal of parenting.

THE TRAVEL IDEAL

When Liz and I travel, we optimize for having authentic experiences and challenging adventures. We eschew tourist infrastructure and instead seek out interesting experiences off the beaten path. We make every meal count by finding restaurants frequented by locals or touted by reviewers; it's like we can smell a menu printed in multiple languages. We put ourselves in new situations that require us to rise to the challenge—whether rappelling down waterfalls in Vietnam, navigating the public bus system across Croatia, or hitchhiking in Norway.

THE PARENTING IDEAL

With our kids, we optimize for parenting in a way that balances respect for them with providing safe and loving boundaries. We optimize the schedule for their rhythms. We focus on child-led activities rather than dictating what they do. We adjust the space to be as focused on "yes" as possible, taking away dangers and distractions that require a constant barrage of "no." When possible, we let their choices lead the way.

When looking at our two ideals, we realize it's impossible to travel the way we'd like to travel while parenting. And, it's impossible to parent the way we'd like to parent while traveling.

So, back to the question at hand. How is it on the road with two little ones?

I find that I am grateful for the beautiful travel moments I can steal while taking care of these two. That brief moment sitting under the pounding of the hot springs waterfall. The tropical fruits and sips of Costa Rican coffee before a long mealtime implodes. The massage in an open-air bungalow and speedy zipline tour while my wife takes care of the little ones.

At the same time, I am grateful for the beautiful parenting moments I can steal while traveling. Playing telemarketer on the unplugged hotel room phone with my toddler. Making finger puppet shapes on the ceiling to entertain my newborn. Long talks about where things go when you flush the toilet and unexpected potty-training wins.

Yet, what I have been completely caught off guard and delighted by are the new moments of integration in which traveling and parenting transform each other. The best parts of this trip, and undoubtedly the most memorable, are the rare moments when it all happens together in a new and different way. The conversations with my toddler about how mud is made as I carry her through ankle-deep gunk in the jungle. The quiet moments breastfeeding my newborn son while looking out into the tropical rain. The kids' reaction to a handful of white-nosed coatis wandering up to our hotel room window.

By combining the two, the nature of both parenting and traveling changes completely. On the road, I become a different parent. I let go of optimizing their world for respectful, independent learning. I am more flexible and fluid. And with kids in tow, I become a different traveler. I don't need everything to be perfectly authentic and perpetually challenging. I slow down, judge less, and see this place through their eyes.

So, am I eating more hotel hamburgers than I would like? Absolutely. And am I also delaying nap time to fit in one more store, one more museum, or one more dip in the pool? Yes. But, increasingly, instead of feeling as if I am compromising on both sides, I feel I am finding the beautiful integration of both.

What in your life is not how you aspired for it to be because of your commitments?

What is still possible despite your obligations?

What is only possible because of your obligations?

This brings us to the end of Chapter Four, *Surrender*. As we come near the end of the book, I want to take a collective sigh. Seriously. Breathe in through your nose. Breathe out through your mouth and exhale a big "ahhhhh." Let your body symbolically surrender that small bit of breath. Do it again. In through your nose, and exhale with an "ah."

Now, reflect upon these last questions:

What are you holding on to?
How does this holding on impact you?

What do you need to let go of, if only a little bit?
What is holding you back from doing so?

What will you do to begin loosening your grip?

CONCLUSION

A conscious awareness, a complementary practice of reflection, an on-going endeavor to align action, and a willingness to surrender are the best tools I have found to live intentionally. Yet, there's much more to be written on the topic of intentionality and even more to be experienced.

I hope that after sharing these essays and experiences together, this book feels like an old friend. I hope that you see more clearly. I hope that you feel called to live differently. I hope that intentionality has a different meaning to you, one that is truer, deeper, more challenging and yet more inviting.

As you move forward, I ask you to commit to just one thing you will do differently—just one tiny step in the direction of intentionality. Keep in mind as you do this, you do not have to be perfect. Your actions and ambitions do not have to be in unwavering alignment at all times. What matters, now and in the future, is that you commit to some small action in the world and, then, consciously and continuously live the questions of intentionality. Keep them front of mind: *What do I want? What am I doing?* and *What am I becoming?* Your action may be derailed. You may not come to answers—not soon, and perhaps not at all. And yet, over time, you will come to see the landscape of your life more clearly, reflect upon what you find, and act in alignment with your ambitions. Then, simply judge for yourself how it feels to live more intentionally.

I wish you clarity and meaning in your pursuit of an intentional life.

DO YOU WANT TO CONTINUE THE CONVERSATION?

I am excited to continue the dialogue about intentionality and to support each other in living more consciously. To that end, I have listed a number of resources available to you below; all are accessible at www.meredithwhipplecallahan.com.

- **Download the free discussion guide.**
  You will find more resources about *The Intentional Life*, including a free discussion guide, on my website. This discussion guide is a starting point for group discussions about the book.
- **Invite me to your book club.** If your book club reads *The Intentional Life*, feel free to invite me along. Though I'm not always available in person, I am often able to do a Skype or Zoom call, which enables us to have a live chat. I always learn something and benefit from hearing your experience of intentionality.

- **Engage me formally**. I am also available for more formal events, including speaking engagements, workshops, and facilitated discussions.
- **Share your thoughts**. Even if only via email, I am excited to continue the dialogue together. Reach out to me with questions, thoughts, disagreements, and suggestions. In fact, the more critical your feedback, the more welcome it will be. The only way the dialogue about intentionality will progress is by hearing and integrating different—and, often, dissenting—points of view.

www.meredithwhipplecallahan.com

DO YOU WANT TO READ MORE FROM MEREDITH WHIPPLE CALLAHAN?

My first book, *Indispensable: How to Succeed at Your First Job and Beyond*, outlines how employees early in their careers can maximize their potential in the workplace. Though a book on career advice for young professionals may seem quite different from a book about conscious living, the origins are the same. In each case, the book was born from my reflections upon life as I experienced it—in that case, as a young professional finding most opportunities for personal evolution in the workplace. I have included the Preface and Introduction to that book here as bonus material.

PREFACE

The idea for *Indispensable* came when I left my job at Bain & Company and prepared to attend Stanford Graduate School of Business. Taking my first break from work as a professional adult, I had time and space to reflect on the early years of my career. While I was proud of my trajectory of strong performance and stellar reviews, I also knew that my success was not the result of my hard work alone. I had learned so much through Bain's formal and informal training. I was also the lucky beneficiary of exceptional mentorship over the years. This got me thinking: What advice would I pass along to someone starting the path I just walked? What had I learned that was universal and transferrable?"

I clawed back through the journals I kept during my early professional years and reflected upon what made me successful. I dug for insight from not only my own experiences but those of others. I conducted dozens of interviews with successful junior employees, managers of junior employees, and leaders in the talent space. I ran an online survey of over 175 employees to understand what made them and others successful in the workplace. Beyond this—and perhaps most importantly—I sat down with innumerable friends and colleagues who had been star performers in high-profile entry-level jobs, hashing out what advice they received and what they learned along the way. Finally, as the insights began to emerge, I collaborated with half a dozen talented MBAs and PhDs to check that the key points applied broadly, across industries. From my own experience and that of others, I started to pull together the essential puzzle pieces that would help employees to perform exceptionally.

The result was *Indispensable*. As you will see, this is not an academic tract on what makes employees successful. It is not the result of quantitative analysis or statistical proofs, nor is it a redaction of other workplace advice. Instead, *Indispensable* is a synthesis of real-life experiences in some of the most prestigious and challenging entry-level jobs out there.

I wish you the best in your work life, and I hope you find *Indispensable* useful. For those of you starting your careers, the advice here is meant to accelerate you along your path. For those of you later in your careers, I hope this prompts you to reflect on what made you successful along the way—whether it was by these strategies or others—and to emerge better equipped to mentor the next generation of employees.

For more information or to engage further in the *Indispensable* conversation, visit my website, www.indispensablebook.com. I appreciate your input and know that it will help make the next edition of this book even broader and richer.

INTRODUCTION

You are not the typical employee. You are not satisfied by merely eking out an existence. You refuse to execute your tasks mindlessly. You cannot get excited about hurrying through the week as you wait for the weekend.

No, you have higher ambitions and better prospects. You want to be challenged and engaged. You want to excel at your job. In addition to promotions, raises, and the corner office (or whatever indicates success in your chosen field), you want respect, autonomy, and satisfaction. In short, you want to prove that you are so talented, so effective, and so helpful that you are considered *indispensable* by your organization. But how to begin? Work long hours? Cross all your t's and dot all your i's? Buy the boss a muffin basket?

Indispensable: How to Succeed at Your First Job and Beyond provides direction for becoming the best employee you can be. Whether you're starting a new job, meeting a new manager, or taking on a new assignment, *Indispensable* gives you the strategies you need to excel. Over twelve chapters, this book outlines the characteristics of indispensable employees and gives practical solutions for developing each skill.

WHY YOU SHOULD CARE

What is meaningful about becoming indispensable? Why is it worth the effort? The benefits of indispensability include more security in your current role, greater satisfaction and fulfillment in the workplace, and better professional opportunities in the future.

The most basic benefit of becoming indispensable is exactly that: indispensability. When the economy takes a dive, pink slips materialize and long-term job security disappears. In tough times, distinguishing yourself from the pack helps preserve your paycheck. Becoming indispensable also helps prevent underemployment, a state in which you may settle for a job that demands less than you are able to contribute. As an indispensable employee, you are more likely to have and keep the job that fits your skills and ambitions.

That said, the intangible benefits of indispensability are even more rewarding; not only do indispensable employees have jobs, they are more likely to enjoy their jobs. Smart organizations know that employees seek engagement at the highest level; workers want a sense of purpose, the opportunity to contribute, inclusion in a community, and the support to learn and develop. Indispensable employees are more likely to realize all these aspirations. You are given more interesting and important work. You are entrusted to tackle that work autonomously, minimizing the need for close management. Ultimately, as an indispensable employee, you are more likely to be not just satisfied with your job but delighted by it.

It is shortsighted to count the benefits of indispensability to your current situation alone. Ultimately, indispensability pays off with the opportunity to learn and grow in both this role and the next. Becoming indispensable allows you to accelerate your career path and, more importantly, to accelerate your professional growth. Positive performance assessments give indispensable employees leverage to secure plum new projects, and satisfied managers are more likely to suggest indispensable employees for promotions. And, while they may not be able to imagine life without them, managers are also more likely to provide positive references for indispensable employees when they move on to another organization. Thus, though *Indispensable* may appear to be about becoming indispensable to one manager, the book helps you become indispensable along your entire career path, reaping the tangible and intangible benefits along the way.

HOW THIS BOOK IS ORGANIZED

Despite the great variety of jobs out there, the qualifications many companies tend to look for in their junior employees are remarkably similar. Most professional jobs require a similar set of essential skills focused around organization, problem solving, communication, and teamwork. Thus, whether you are designing furniture or balancing the books, a common set of strategies will help you become excellent.

Indispensable is split into three sections that cover this suite of skills: Nail the Basics, Excel at Execution, and Exceed Expectations. These sections are organized to build in both chronology (from skills you can demonstrate at the beginning to those you can show later) and complexity (from simpler skills to more complex skills).

First, you **nail the basics**. These are the underlying requirements for not only becoming an indispensable employee but being a functional worker. Toward this end, you present yourself professionally, adopt a great attitude, and invest yourself in the mission of your organization. You also seek out information about your position, organization, and industry, understanding this information will be useful as you progress. You are thoughtful about starting strong and setting yourself up for long-term success. Remembering that reputations are set early and become hard to change, you demonstrate these indispensable traits from day one. Chapters 1–4 help you lay that foundation.

Second, you **excel at execution**. As you tackle your work, you take pains to execute even the least interesting of tasks in an efficient and error-free manner. You know that reliability is a prerequisite for more responsibility. Then, as you gain experience, you execute your job better and better. You finish your work well and communicate effectively. You bravely address problems and tackle interpersonal issues. Task by task, you prove yourself, building confidence and earning trust. Chapters 5–9 help you prove your competence and excel at the tasks within your scope.

Finally, you **exceed expectations.** As an indispensable employee, you do more than is asked of you. Instead of sticking to your narrow job description, you make an impact beyond those particular responsibilities. You stretch to take on more responsibility. You take the initiative to improve your organization broadly. You also proactively push your own professional development, going beyond the formal feedback processes to drive your growth. Chapters 10–12 lay out strategies for going beyond excellent execution and exceeding all expectations. This is the realm of becoming fully indispensable; here you lay the groundwork to advance from an indispensable employee to a manager and leader of others.

HOW TO USE THIS BOOK

Each chapter of *Indispensable* focuses on one aspect of work and proposes four or five essential strategies for doing that well. Each of these strategies also includes a set of "Indispensable Solutions," practical suggestions that help you apply that strategy more tangibly. Collectively, this means that there are more than fifty strategies of becoming indispensable.

Given this number of strategies, you may wonder where to start and how to prioritize your time. It is important to know that no single strategy is more important than the others. While you need not display every quality all of the time, indispensability comes from bringing a strong suite of skills to your organization. To get the most out of *Indispensable*, read through all the strategies and consider how each one applies to you. The more dimensions of yourself you can develop, the more likely you are to be indispensable and to find the satisfaction that comes with that.

That said, a subset of these strategies is likely to be most relevant to your current role at this moment in time. Jobs are different; developing a marketing campaign for Coca-Cola in Pondicherry is unlike designing apps in Denver. Similarly, bosses are different; one looks for concise communication while another wants to ensure that you cover all the details.

Though you develop yourself broadly (for this job and the next), you may want to focus on only a couple of strategies today. Think critically about what handful of strategies is most pertinent at this moment—to both your current situation and your personal development.

As you progress, you will also apply the indispensable strategies in a way that is more and more consistent with your unique style and personality. For example, while some of the conflict-management approaches would sound very natural coming from one person, they could seem insincere when used by another (see chapter 9, "Take On Conflict Productively"). Similarly, different employees may find themselves endorsing the mission of their organization in different ways; one employee may wear the company's motto on her sleeve, while another may quietly but sincerely ascribe to its values (see chapter 3, "Invest Yourself in the Mission"). The indispensable strategies are yours to use. Do not subsume yourself and your unique personality to these strategies; endeavor to make them yours over time.

Of course, all of this will take work. You cannot passively read this book and reap the benefits. This does not necessarily mean you work longer hours than others, but you will apply yourself more intentionally than those around you. You will approach your work in a more thoughtful way, considering what you are doing and why. You will dedicate yourself to not only the tasks of your job but also to the self-development work that accompanies personal growth. As you likely already guessed, there are no tips, tricks, or shortcuts to exceling at your job. Instead, becoming indispensable requires the development of skills over time. Though you may have to focus your development on only a handful of strategies at a time, you will eventually build a portfolio of ways that you are indispensable. To get the most out of *Indispensable*, you need to commit to making that investment.

Remember: You are not the typical employee. You have higher aspirations. And now you have in your hand the practical playbook for becoming excellent at your job, happier in your workplace, and indispensable to your organization. By opening this book and beginning the journey, you are already on track to becoming your best self at work. Enjoy the journey toward becoming indispensable.

Indispensable: How to Succeed at Your First Job and Beyond is available in paperback and eBook formats from Amazon, Barnes and Noble, and Indiebound.

ACKNOWLEDGMENTS

Thank you to everyone who supported *The Intentional* over its first five years and also to everyone who helped this volume come into existence. In particular, I am grateful for the following:

Elizabeth Callahan: Liz, since the beginning, you have been instrumental in helping me put *The Intentional* out into the world, supporting me with your developmental editing, your social marketing savvy, and your partnership (or, more appropriately, leadership) on the home front.

Mike McKay: You have been next to me throughout this journey, present as I wrestle with the uncertainty, fear, and self-doubt that writing prompts. I appreciate that, whoever else reads each post, I know that I have a thoughtful consumer in you. I always look forward to your emails and our chats.

Hugh Archer Whipple Callahan: In my first book, *Indispensable: How to Succeed at Your First Job and Beyond*, I thanked your sister, Elliott Claire. I was inspired to return to writing in a serious way during my maternity leave with her. This time around, for my second book, you were my muse. I am grateful for all the cuddles while I worked on the manuscript. Over the handful of months you've been with us, you have already shown me the way to greater love.

Victoria Hunter: Hearing the impact of *Indispensable* on your life inspired me to make *The Intentional Life* as powerful as it could be. Thank you for seeing and sharing the ambitious vision that you had for my writing. Your partnership in re-envisioning this book was essential to making it what it is.

Everyone who lent their expertise to this book: In particular, I want to thank my editor Bonnie Hearn Hill, my audiobook coach Sean Pratt, my cover designer Noel Lee, and my interior designer Sarah Beaudin. I also want to thank the team at Elephant Audiobooks for bringing the audiobook version to life. Finally, thanks to the Potrero Press team for escorting me through this process. I am grateful for partnerships like ours in which we are all committed to the cause and can bring our different talents to our common work.

My readers Eleanore Douglas, Moshe Ovadia, Tim Kleiman, David Whipple, and Janice Whipple: Thank you for being on the front lines as *The Intentional Life* came together as a book. I am grateful for your willingness to make the time to read it, provide your critiques, and, moreover, share your love as this became real.

All my supporters and subscribers: Thank you for your enthusiasm and support throughout. I am encouraged by all of you who subscribe to the emails, post comments, and like the links. Thank you for keeping me going.

And, finally, **Ann Frisby Callahan**: I am grateful that *The Intentional* gave you a greater window into me and prompted deeper discussion between us. You taught me more than you know. You are loved and missed.

POTRERO
P R E S S

Potrero Press publishes books with the potential to have significant impact on how we think about living well as humans. Based outside of New York City, we focus on books that address topics of personal evolution, leadership development, human potential, and meaning.

The goat on Potrero Press's logo represents the values and aspirations we hold dear. Goats are independent adventurers who don't hesitate to scale high heights. Seeking ever higher terrain, they represent boldness, capability, ambition, and spiritual exploration. Similarly, books bearing the Potrero Press imprint bring big, life-changing messages to readers in a way that is elegant and easily accessible.

We love to be in community with readers, fans, and potential new authors. You can find more about us and get in touch at www.potreropress.com.

59057171R10131

Made in the USA
Columbia, SC
01 June 2019